HOODOO—a word many have he...
Hoodoo magick is a blend of Eu...
magic brought to the New Wo...
Hoodoo is a *folk magic* that can be learned and easily mastered by anyone.

In this book, Ray Malbrough reveals to you the secrets of Hoodoo magick. By using the simple materials available in Nature, you can bring about the necessary changes to greatly benefit your life and that of your friends. You are given detailed instructions for making and using the *gris-gris* (charm) bags only casually or mysteriously mentioned by other writers. Malbrough not only shows how to make gris-gris bags for health, money, luck, love and protection from evil and harm, etc., but he also explains how these charms work.

He also takes you into the world of *doll magick;* using dolls in rituals to gain love, success, or prosperity. Complete instructions are given for making the dolls and setting up the ritual.

There is genuine pleasure in the making of your own anointing oils, sprinkling powders, ritual incenses, etc. Here are complete formulas for making and using them in simple *spell-casting* for attracting love, protection, prophetic dreams, luck, success and more.

Always the tools of Hoodoo magick are simple, inexpensive, easily found and easily used. A simple oil lamp can be turned into an instrument which will help bring to reality your desires for justice in court dealings, finding employment, and fulfilling simple basic needs.

Hoodoo magick can be as enjoyable as it is practical, and in this fascinating book you can learn how to be a *practitioner*, working your spells and charms for yourself or for others. Learn the methods which have been used successfully by Hoodoo practitioners for nearly 200 years, along with many practical tips for dealing with your clients.

Hoodoo is magick *anyone* can do.

About the Author

Ray T. Malbrough was born in New Orleans and was raised in the "Pays des Cajuns" region of southeastern Louisiana. He learned the basics of Hoodoo in his early teens with the permission and encouragement of his mother. At age 19, he started working in a New Orleans tearoom as a reader/advisor, and has since earned a good reputation as a Hoodoo worker all over the region surrounding his hometown of Houma. He is a 1982 graduate of the Seax-Wica Seminary founded and directed by Dr. Raymond Buckland. The author is active in the Parapsychology Association in Thibodeaux, Louisiana. Today, Ray is a full time reader/advisor and Hoodoo worker in his home in Houma.

To Write to the Author

If you wish to contact the author or would like more information about this book, please write to the author in care of Llewellyn Worldwide, and we will forward your request. Both the author and publisher appreciate hearing from you and learning of your enjoyment of this book and how it has helped you. Llewellyn Worldwide cannot guarantee that every letter written to the author can be answered, but all will be forwarded. Please write to:

Ray T. Malbrough
c/o Llewellyn Worldwide
P.O. Box 64383-501, St. Paul, MN 55164-0383, U.S.A.

Please enclose a self-addressed, stamped envelope for reply, or $1.00 to cover costs. If outside the U.S.A., enclose international postal reply coupon.

Free Catalog from Llewellyn

For more than 90 years Llewellyn has brought its readers knowledge in the fields of metaphysics and human potential. Learn about the newest books in spiritual guidance, natural healing, astrology, occult philosophy and more. Enjoy book reviews, new age articles, a calendar of events, plus current advertised products and services. To get your free copy of *Llewellyn's New Worlds of Mind and Spirit*, send your name and address to:

Llewellyn's New Worlds of Mind and Spirit
P.O. Box 64383-501, St. Paul, MN 55164-0383, U.S.A.

About Llewellyn's Practical Magick Series

To some people, the idea that "Magick" is *practical* comes as a suprise.

It shouldn't. The entire basis for Magick is to exercise influence over one's environment. While Magick is also, and properly so, concerned with spiritual growth and psychological transformation, even the spiritual life must rest firmly on material foundations.

The material world and the psychic are intertwined, and it is this very fact that establishes the Magickal Link: that the psychic can as easily influence the material as vice versa.

Magick can, and should, be used in one's daily life for better living! Each of us has been given Mind and Body, and surely we are under Spiritual obligation to make full usage of these wonderful gifts. Mind and Body work together, and Magick is simply the extension of this interaction into dimensions beyond the limits normally conceived. That's why we commonly talk of the "supernormal" in connection with domain of Magick.

The Body is alive, and all Life is an expression of the Divine. There is God-power in the Body and in the Earth, just as there is in Mind and Spirit. With Love and Will, we use Mind to link these aspects of Divinity together to bring about change.

With Magick we increase the flow of Divinity in our lives and in the world around us. We add to the beauty of it all—for to work Magick we must work in harmony with the Laws of Nature and of the Psyche. *Magick is the flowering of the Human Potential.*

Practical Magick is concerned with the Craft of Living well and in harmony with Nature, and with the Magick of the Earth, in the things of the Earth, in the seasons and cycles and in the things we make with hand and Mind.

Llewellyn's Practical Magick Series

CHARMS, SPELLS & FORMULAS

For the Making and Use of Gris-Gris,
Herb Candles, Doll Magick, Incenses,
Oils and Powders . . . To Gain Love,
Protection, Prosperity, Luck
and Prophetic Dreams

Ray T. Malbrough

1996
Llewellyn Publications
St. Paul, Minnesota 55164-0383, U.S.A.

FIRST EDITION
Fifteenth Printing, 1996

Cover art by Robin Wood
Book design by Terry Buske
Interior illustrations by Nancy Benson

Library of Congress Cataloging-in-Publication Data
Malbrough, Ray.
    Charms, spells, and formulas for the making and use of gris-gris, herb candles, doll magick, incenses, oils, and powders—to gain love, protection, prosperity, luck, and prophetic dreams.

    (Llewellyn's practical magick series)
    1. Folklore—Louisiana. 2. Magic—Louisiana.
3. Charms. 4. Incantations. I. Title. II. Series.
GR110.L5M35   1986   398'.09763   86-45286
ISBN 0-87542-501-1

Llewellyn Publications
A Division of Llewellyn Worldwide, Ltd.
P.O. Box 64383, St. Paul, MN 55164-0383

Specal thanks to Cyndi Hanson, who has shared with me some of her knowledge of formulas.

****

I thank the Seax-Wica Seminary, through which my involvement as a student has encouraged me to share what I have learned concerning the Magickal Practice of my part of the world.

Contents

INTRODUCTION

Since the dawn of man, people of all civilizations have placed their faith in the use of charms and various forms of magickal practice. Methods may have differed from one civilization to the next. And today, in this fast moving technical society, people from all walks of life still use charms and magick in their daily lives.

Occult shops and mail order firms have sprung up all over the country, evidence to man's continued belief in the occult sciences. Today, when you walk into any occult shop you will see shelves of various herbs, incense, anointing oils, powders and washes. Each has its own use and effect. No self-respecting occult shop would be without its supply of candles in all sizes, shapes and colors. Also, you will find books on various aspects of the occult.

Within these pages you will learn a method of making charms and using magick with dolls which have been passed on from teacher to student among the voodoo practitioners in southeast Louisiana. The use of the gris-gris bag is still quite strong, especially in and around the New Orleans area. The use of dolls in making magick is used only in the rural areas of the state. Since the early colonization of Louisiana, voodoo in one form or another has been practiced and feared by people in all walks of life in south Louisiana.

Within these pages you will learn how to make your own incense, anointing oils, powders and washes. Sure these are items which can be bought in any reputable occult shop. But, in the old days, there were no occult shops in which to buy anything related to magick. The practitioners of old almost always had to make everything they used from scratch. With the recipes in this book you will be able to do this. Here you will find a formula to make that special incense, anointing oil, powder, etc. comparable in use to the name brands on the market today. All ingredients used in these formulas can be obtained from any reputable occult shop. Some of the ingredients may even be purchased in most health food stores.

When it comes to anointing oils, it is difficult to get a clear oil. Almost all of the name brand oils on the market are colored red, blue, green, etc. These are fine but the colored oils should be used only on a candle of the same color if you are using the oil to anoint a candle for ritual. Many of the formulas in this book will give you a clear oil, making its use more versatile.

Ray T. Malbrough

Chapter One

WHAT IS MAGICK?

Archeologists, as well as those learned in contemporary religion, clearly point out that a belief in and use of magick (the old English spelling of the word) has existed since man's early history.

Magick was defined by Aleister Crowley as, "The art or science of causing change to occur in conformity with will". And since man is basically motivated by his emotions of love and hate, magick has developed into two forms: one which is motivated to benefit mankind, commonly termed 'white' magick, and that which is geared to injure mankind, termed 'black' magick.

It is usually misconstrued that anyone who successfully practices magick is a witch. This is not true, because magick in itself is a practice. Therefore, anyone may learn and use magick in their life. Such a person is properly referred to as a 'magician'. A witch is a person who belongs to the Old Religion of pre-Christian Europe commonly called witchcraft and often referred to as wicca today.

For those who are seriously interested in learning the truth as to what witchcraft is all about, and in detail, the Saxon tradition of wicca, I strongly recommend you read the forthcoming book from Llewellyn, *Ray Buckland's Complete Course on*

Witchcraft.

There is a law operating in the Universe in which all your actions sooner or later come back to you. Because of this Universal Law at work, a so-called black magician never lives a long, happy and prosperous life. Never be tempted to use your magick to harm another. These actions can only lead you to a future of misery and frustration.

Mankind over the years has developed different forms of magick. In my opinion, the oldest form known is sympathetic magick based on the concept that like attracts like. Then there is ceremonial magick which has its roots in the Jewish system of magick known as the Qabalah. Here the magician conjures up all sorts of entities to do his bidding for him. Many of the entities conjured are very antagonistic toward the magician, so this form of magick can be dangerous. Another form is talismanic magick in which a manmade object is endowed with power or energy to help attract to its wearer the object of his desires. A talisman can also be made to protect from evil.

As I've said there are many methods used to work magick. The three just mentioned are the most popular, used by the lone magician today.

Within these pages it is my intention to teach the method commonly used in southeast Louisiana, the gris-gris bag, which has its roots in voodoo. Also, I illustrate a variation of sympathetic magick as I have learned it, using dolls. Here you will learn to use and make charms and spells which are a part of the lone magician's magick.

Getting Started

Before you will be able to make any of the charms or do any of the rituals as taught in this book, you will need a place to do them. This should be a place that is quiet, a place where you can be alone without fear of being disturbed. If you have your own bedroom, use it. The best place to use is the attic, basement or a spare room where people living in the house do not enter often. Some of the rituals given in this book will take several days to complete, and they must remain undisturbed until then.

Noise is something you should try to eliminate as much as possible. The sound of a radio or stereo playing, the television blasting away, traffic on the street, even the voices of people talking loud, will hinder your success in your rituals. All these outside disturbances only serve to take your undivided attention away from your ritual work. I would also like to add, unplug the telephone.

You will need something to use as an altar to do your ritual work on. Actually, you can use anything—a wooden box, a coffee table, a board resting on cinder blocks. Most people prefer using the top of their chest of drawers, using the top drawer to store away their ritual supplies. On each corner at the back of your altar you will place a white candle. These will be known as your altar candles. The altar candles are traditionally lit in the following order: the candle at your left, first, and the candle at your right, second. If you like, you may cover your altar with a cloth. Your altar cloth should be white. Some people, including myself, like to put flowers on their altar. Flowers tend to remind us of the beauty that is in nature. If you are going to use flowers on your altar, please use fresh cut flowers and not artificial ones. Refer to the basic altar layout.

Many people like to add religious figures or pictures as a part of their altar arrangement. It is not necessary but if you like to do so, these are placed in back of the altar between your altar candles with your incense burner placed in front.

Since incense will be used in all the rituals, you will need an incense burner. If you cannot find an incense burner in the shops in your area, you can make your own. Any noncombustible, heat resistant dish or bowl the size of a cup will do fine. This should be half filled with earth or sand. The earth or sand will absorb the heat generated from the burning incense

4 / Charms, Spells, Formulas

```
┌─────────────────────────────────────────────────┐
│                                                   │
│  Flowers    Altar Candle    Altar Candle   Flowers│
│                                                   │
│                Incense Burner                     │
│                                                   │
│                                                   │
│                                                   │
│                                                   │
│              Book              Holy Water         │
│                                                   │
└─────────────────────────────────────────────────┘
```

Basic Altar Layout

and will prevent scorching your altar. The recipes for making the incense used are given in Part II of this book.

In the rituals we will be using various colored candles. Each color has been given its own vibratory influence. Since only the color is important, it makes no difference as to the size or shape of the candle. The colors we will be working with and their vibratory influences are:

WHITE..Adds to spiritual strength, breaks curses or crossed conditions, represents faith, purity, truth and sincerity.

PINK..Overcomes evil, represents honor, love, morality, friendship, general success.

RED..Love, sexuality, good health, strength and physical vigor.

ORANGE......................................Encouragement, strengthens the ability to concentrate, attraction, adaptability, stimulation.

YELLOW.................................Attraction, persuasion (can change minds), instills confidence, charm.

GREEN...................................Money, luck, financial success and prosperity, fertility, good crops and harvest, cooperation.

LIGHT BLUE..........................Understanding, health, tranquility, protection, peace, general happiness, sharpens the power to perceive, spiritual awareness, patience.

DARK BLUE...........................Depression, moodiness, changeability, impulsiveness, unfortunate and very subduing.

PURPLE.................................Ambition, promotes business progress, power (worldly, psychic or magickal), causes tension, strengthens willpower.

BROWN.................................Hesitation in all matters, uncertainty and doubt, neutrality, robs energy.

BLACK...................................Sadness and mourning, evil, loss, discord, confusion.

GRAY.....................................Cancellation, stalemate, neutrality.

GREENISH YELLOW.............Jealousy and anger, sickness, quarrels, discord, cowardice.

To give added strength to the vibratory influences of the candles in ritual they should be first "Blessed" to remove any negative vibrations and dirt, then "Dressed" to set firmly the desired vibrations you want in your ritual. The manner for "blessing" is given in the section titled "Preliminary to Ritual".

"Dressing" is the term most often used to mean anointing the candle with oil. Dressing the candle is done in the following procedure. Starting from the center of the candle, rub your oil on the candle's surface with your right hand (left, if left-handed) upward to the candle's wick. Continue rubbing the oil on the candle's surface, from the center upwards until the entire top half of the candle is anointed. Then from the candle's center, rub downward to the bottom of the candle. Continue rubbing the oil from the center downward until the bottom half of the candle's surface is anointed. It is very, very important that you concentrate upon the symbolism which the candle has in your ritual while you are anointing it. The act of concentration while anointing the candle with oil firmly sets in the mind of the operator the vibratory influence which the candle will have during the ritual. To further fix in your mind the symbolism the candle has in your ritual, hold the candle in your right hand (left, if left-handed) and visualize the candle's symbolism. If the candle represents money, see money or the amount you need, if love—a heart, etc. .

When to do Your Rituals

When you are going to do a ritual it is wise to consider the phases of the moon. All rituals of a constructive nature such as: love, success, progress, fertility, health, improvement, to change jobs, to prevent evil, wealth, etc., should be done when the moon is waxing. The moon is said to be waxing from

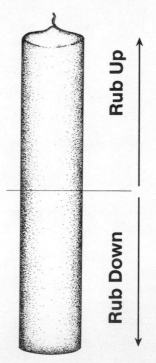

Rub Up

Rub Down

the period between the New Moon to the Full Moon. All rituals of a destructive nature such as: ending a love affair, to stop another from doing a certain act, putting a stop to bad habits, to cause discord, etc., should be done during the waning phase of the moon. The period from the Full Moon to the New Moon is the waning phase of the Moon.

As you can see, we are going to give our rituals some extra help by doing them during certain phases of the moon. We will also enlist the aid of seven planets. Each day of the week is ruled by one of the seven planets. Each planet is said to have an influence over certain matters concerning our daily lives. The days of the week with their planetary rulers are as follows:

SUNDAY .... Is ruled by the Sun. The color associated with Sunday is yellow. Sunday's influence concerns creating peace and harmony, obtaining the favor of those in high places, (this can even mean your boss or immediate supervisor at work), riches, honor, glory, making friends, recovering lost property, preventing war.

MONDAY .... Is ruled by the Moon. Its associated color is white. Monday is good to begin rituals for reconciliations, dreams, receptivity, love, voyages (to encourage good or safe), messages, female fertility.

TUESDAY .... Is ruled by Mars. The color associated with Mars is red. The positive influence of Mars concerns developing courage, overthrowing enemies, military honors, breaking negative spells. In the negative aspect, Mars can create strife and hardships, cause bitterness between friendships, etc.

WEDNESDAY .... Is ruled by Mercury. Its associated color is purple. Mercury's influence concerns health, science, studies, psychic and spiritual development, communications, divination, influencing others.

THURSDAY.......... Is ruled by Jupiter. The color associated with Thursday is blue. Use this day to begin your rituals concerning wealth, obtaining honors, male fertility, friendship, health, to obtain luck, success in your chosen career, general ambition.

FRIDAY.................. Is ruled by the planet Venus. Its associated color is green. Venus' influence in our lives deals with love, romance, beauty, kindness, happiness, travel, to foster new friendships, to gratify lust.

SATURDAY........... Is ruled by the planet Saturn. The color associated with Saturn is black. Saturn's influence is for psychic attack (its negative side), psychic self-defense (its positive aspect), to protect from evil, spirit communication, and anything connected with the home.

Let us suppose that you have just begun a new job and you want to do some ritual work to build a good relationship with your boss. This would be considered constructive magick and would have a greater chance of success done during the waxing phase of the moon. Now we are going to look at the calendar to be sure what phase of the moon we are in at present. We see that the New Moon occurred five days ago. Therefore we are already in the correct phase of the moon and do not have to wait. Now we consult our table of influences for the days of the week. We see that the sun is associated with the gaining of favor from those in high places and it is also good for making friends. From this information we know that Sunday is good to begin this particular ritual. We therefore go back to our calendar to find out how many days we will have to wait until Sunday arrives during the waxing phase of the moon to begin our ritual. During this short waiting period we can gather together all the materials that will be needed in order to perform the ritual.

Now comes the question: at what time of the day should I do my ritual work? The simple solution to this question is to do your rituals at either the first hour of sunrise or the first hour of sunset. Whichever time you decide upon, it is important to do your ritual work at the same time each consecutive day until the ritual is complete.

Preliminary to Ritual

The first step is to eliminate anything which will interrupt you and invade your privacy during the ritual. If it makes you feel more secure, lock the door to the room where you are doing your ritual work. An ordinary screen door hook can be attached to the door if you so desire.

Set up your altar according to the basic altar layout. Gather all the materials that you will be using in your ritual. All materials used in each ritual will be listed as I give each ritual in detail. These items may be placed on a small table next to the altar. Double check to make sure that you have not forgotten something. Also you will need a special "Psychic and Spiritual Development Herb Candle". On this candle write your full name and birthdate. Dress the herb candle with "Power Oil".

Turn out the lights so that you will be surrounded by the natural darkness of the room.

Step 1. Light your altar candles. Light your incense.

Step 2. Light the special "Psychic and Spiritual Development Herb Candle".

Step 3. Anoint your forehead with "Power Oil" by making a cross. Imagine a bright white light beaming down upon you and filling you from head to toe. See this white light expand and surround you. See it growing in size to completely fill the room. Know in your mind that you are filled with and surrounded by this light and no power of darkness can hurt you in any way.

Step 4. Take the bowl of holy water and with your fingers sprinkle all the corners of the room, then on and around your altar area, saying:

> Where this holy water is cast,
> no spell or thing of darkness lasts,
> that's not in harmony with me,
> From this moment you must flee.

When finished, place the bowl of holy water back on the altar.

Step 5. Meditate for a moment upon the intention for doing your ritual.

These steps I've just mentioned are to be performed before every ritual. Steps 3 and 4 act as a cleansing of yourself and the area where you will be doing your work. Plus, these actions will help to remove any negativity which could interfere with the success of your work.

As you are setting up your altar to begin your ritual, it will be necessary to consecrate (or bless) everything you will use as you place it on the altar. This is done only once, so there is no need to repeat this step daily.

Dip your fingers in the holy water and touch the item with the holy water with the words:

> Through this holy water pure,
> no negativity endures.
> Consecrated as you should,
> be dedicated for the good.

Holy water can be obtained from any Roman Catholic church, or, you can make your own which will be just as effective:

Step 1. Put a tablespoon of salt in a saucer. Place both hands, palms down, over the salt. Mentally direct your energy to flow and say:

> *May this salt be pure and*
> *that the purity of this salt*
> *bless all that it touches.*

Step 2. Place both hands, palms down, over your bowl of water. Mentally direct your energy to flow and say:

> *I consecrate this water that*
> *all negative conditions be*
> *cast out of this water and*
> *I may safely use this water*
> *in my rites.*

Step 3. Stir some of the salt into your water while affirming:

> *Together, this salt and water*
> *will become a powerful instrument*
> *to purify and cast out all evil*
> *and negativity as I use this*
> *holy water in my rites.*

Closing the Ritual

Before you extinguish the altar candles, it is a good idea to pause for a moment to give thanks. Hold your hands with the palms facing towards the altar candles while giving thanks:

> *Thanks for all the blessings*
> *which have touched my life in*
> *the past. I thank you for all*
> *the blessings I know will come*
> *my way in the future, as I*
> *live each day in peace and love.*

Extinguish the candles in the reverse order of lighting them.

NOTE: Steps 1 through 5 are excellent as a ritual for daily prayer. In this case you would burn "Aura of Enchantment Incense". When the period of meditation and prayer is finished, simply close the ritual.

Chapter Two

CHARMS

Charms take the form of what is called gris-gris (pronounced 'gree-gree') bags. This is what they are called in Louisiana. But, this method of making charms is not exclusive to Louisiana. In fact, they are called by different names in various parts of the world—conjure bags, ouanga bags, medicine bags, charm bags, mojo bags, etc. Regardless of the name used, these are small red flannel or chamois drawstring bags, two inches wide and three inches long.

Into the gris-gris bag goes a variety of items; herbs, roots, powders, stones, pieces of colored cloth or feathers, bones, symbols for luck or love or money. Personal items belonging to the individual for whom the gris-gris bag is made are also added: hair, nail parings, pieces of soiled clothing containing perspiration, even discarded Kleenex tissues could be used. The number of items always used to make a gris-gris bag are one, three, five, seven, nine or thirteen. No more than thirteen and never an even number.

The gris-gris bag is a form of talismanic magick in itself and is always made through ritual at an altar. A properly made and consecrated gris-gris bag, when worn by the individual, is believed to help attract or dispel from the person certain influences. Thus, the gris-gris bag can be made for many purposes, good and evil: love, money, health, even to cause sickness, bad luck, or death to an enemy.

To make a gris-gris bag for a woman who desires the love of a certain gentleman, you would use the following: a small heart made from red wax containing hair or other items from both the lady and man of her affections; love-drawing powder; a piece of orris root; vervain; a teaspoon of passion flower. As stated before, construction of the gris-gris bag is done through ritual. All items are to be consecrated at your altar as they are put into the bag. Once the bag is complete it is anointed with oil. Since this bag is made for love, you would use either "love oil" or "attraction oil" or a mixture of both oils.

Now that the lady's gris-gris bag is completed, it is given to her to wear. Women will wear the gris-gris bag pinned to the inside of their bra or inside their dress or blouse near the left armpit. Men usually wear the gris-gris bag around their neck or pinned inside their underwear. Sometimes men will just carry the gris-gris bag in their pocket, so that each time they reach in their pocket the bag will come in contact with their skin.

The woman will also be given a bottle of the same oil that was used in making the gris-gris bag to sprinkle on her bag once a week.

The gris-gris bag, as with any other talisman or amulet, acts as a psycho-spiritual support; it implies faith. It serves to intensify the faith in yourself that through the help of the gris-gris bag you will obtain this or receive that. In order to strengthen your faith in the effectiveness of the gris-gris bag, there must be a complete understanding of what each item you put into your gris-gris bag symbolizes. This is important because the items used act as a psychological aid to strengthen the link between the desire and the mind of the individual whose energy will be used in making the gris-gris bag.

Faith alone is not enough. One must be patient. Patient,

because not all desires will materialize quickly. Some will take time to materialize, in all probability, because certain conditions must be created before the desire can become reality. But if you hold onto your faith and remain patient, the gris-gris bag can serve as a key to open the door to your future happiness.

It has been said that thoughts are things. Human thought produces energy, and the energy creates the force which in turn produces the action. Your will is the operator and director which transmits and guides your thoughts toward their destination. Thus your thoughts, always guided and controlled by your will, become a force that neither time nor distance can deter. All your thoughts, therefore, produce mental vibrations which cannot become lost. In making a gris-gris bag, a certain thought pattern is created and set into motion.

Here I would like to say that the greater your ability to concentrate, the greater success you will obtain in your efforts. You should know how and be able to maintain a fixed thought on a single subject to the exclusion of all other thoughts. This faculty requires training in a calm and isolated atmosphere. With a few minutes of concentration on a determined subject, you will notice that your thoughts begin to wander. Therefore it will be necessary to continue in training yourself to concentrate until you can do so for a period of twenty minutes. For example, select a circle or any other symbol. On the first day of your training in concentration, write down the length of time you were able to hold a clear image of the chosen symbol in your mind. For each day afterwards try to hold the image of the symbol one minute longer, until you can do so for twenty consecutive minutes. It is necessary that you concentrate on the symbol only and push all other thoughts out of your mind; if you are not doing this, you are not training yourself to concentrate on one thing at a time.

Not only should you learn to concentrate, but you should learn to create mental images. The Creative Thought is that which makes concrete a particular subject, which is composed of an exact mental image, with all the relevant characteristics. Through your imagination you should solidly depict in your mind the most exact image possible of the thing that you desire.

Do you want to improve your business? Make a mental picture of your clients crowding and waiting in front of your store before your business hours begin. Imagine all these people buying your merchandise without haggling over your prices. Do you want money? Create the image of the amount of money you want and hold this image in your mind until you can see it materialize in front of you. The clearer your mental images are and the more they are concentrated on with force and intensity, the sooner they will become tangible realities. The vibrations continue emanating from your mind to the ether surrounding you, which creates a magnetic effect that attracts the desired object. You don't need to see where or how you will come into the money; the Universal Mind will choose the proper and just way which will give you the object you're asking for without harming anyone.

It is possible to think without the use of words; it is then that the mental image becomes concrete thought and transforms itself into true Creative Thought. Each thing that you desire actually exists in the surrounding Universe and you can possess it.

In the construction of your gris-gris bags you will be working with herbs. Therefore, it is a good idea to learn which herbs are in harmony with your personality and work only with these in making your gris-gris bags. To find out if an herb is in harmony with you or not, simply hold your left hand over the herb (right, if you are left-handed) and mentally ask the herb, root or bark if it is in harmony with you. If the herb is in harmony with you, you will feel a tingle or flow of energy between your hand and the plant. If you are not in harmony with each other, you will feel nothing at all. Those who are familiar with the use of the pendulum may find its use equally suitable.

The following is a list of herbs and their basic associations. Study this list carefully.

LOVE.....................Cubeb berries, orris root, spikenard, vanillin, vervain, violet flowers, laurel, Adam and Eve root, Beth root, horse chestnut, khus khus, ladies thumb, lavender, lotus, lovage, magnolia, mistletoe, passion flower, patchouli leaves, lesser periwinkle, queen Elizabeth root, quassia chips, rose buds, herba mate, sweet bugle, scullcap, rose hips, orange blossoms, five-finger grass, linden flowers, gentian root, couch grass, heartease herb.

PASSION ....Myrtle, absinthe, aloes, cloves, damiana, dill seed, coriander, dulse herb, sweet basil, juniper berries, saw palmetto berries, Canada snake root, fennel seed, grains of paradise, satyrion root, snake root, verbena root, licorice stick herb, patchouli leaves.

MONEY ....Buckeye, clover, fenugreek, high John the Conqueror root, low John the Conqueror root, nutmeg, marjoram, ruler's root, smartweed, tonka bean, thyme, bayberry herb, echinacea, five-finger grass, Guinea paradise seeds, Irish moss, kelp, lemon verbena, scented lucky beans, silver weed, comfrey, coltsfoot, black snake root, rattlesnake root.

LUCK ....Alfalfa, angel's turnip, ash tree leaves, basil, blessed thistle, chamomile, galangal root, grains of paradise, mustard seed, peony, yellow dock, wonder of the world root, Jezebel root, May apple (mandrake) root, little John chew, tonka beans, Irish moss, queen of the meadow root, quince seeds, parsley, five-finger grass, swiss leaves, silver weed, seven barks, sacred bark, John the conqueror root, four leaf clover, Jamaica ginger root, rosemary, sumbul root.

SUCCESS ....Cinnamon, yellow dock, squill root, John the conqueror root, silver weed, Jezebel root, prince's pine, red clover, buckeye, Irish moss, five-finger grass, elm bark, khus khus, May apple (mandrake) root, scented lucky beans, tonka beans, sweet flag root, vervain leaves, golden seal herb.

HEALTH ....Vervain, thyme, sassafras leaves (and root), peppermint, horehound, hops, eucalyptus, feverfew, asafaetida, catnip, dandelion leaves, sarsaparilla, life everlasting, holy herbs, heal-all herb, golden seal herb, betony, hyssop, pumpkin seed.

PROTECTION .....Vetivert, boldo leaves, mandrake root, gar-
FROM EVIL   lic, snakehead, gilead buds (balm of), stone root, basil leaves, bay leaves, asafaetida, quince seeds, lucky hand root, five-finger grass, dragon's blood reed, blood root, brimstone, frankincense, high John the conqueror root, sacred bark, Saint John's wort, African ginger root, black cohosh, grape vine, fern, rattlesnake root, plant of peace, wolfbane root, caraway seeds.

CURSING ....Balmony root, blueberry, cruel man of the woods, Guinea pepper, knot grass, black mustard seed, pepper tree leaves, poke root, poppy seed, rue, tormentilia, twich's grass, valerian, wormwood, chicory root, flaxseed, jimson weed, mullein, red chincona bark, skunk cabbage root, yohimbee root, pepperwort.

PSYCHIC & ....Five-finger grass, anise seed, burning bush,
SPIRITUAL celery seed, lemon balm, gotu kola, mug-
DEVELOPMENT wort, acacia, marjoram, parsley, cinnamon, mint, thyme, sage, rosemary,
frankincense, bethel root, buchu leaves,
bugle weed, calendula flowers, eyebright
herb.

By studying the list of herbs and their occult associations you will notice that some herbs have more than one association attached to it.

I have made mention that stones can be used to put into the gris-gris bag. For years stones have been given astrological associations and occult properties of attraction. As with the herbs, some authorities may differ. I can only give you the information as I have learned it.* Some people don't use the stones at all, and some find that the use of stones helps to increase the effectiveness of the gris-gris bag. When I started learning the magickal practices in southern Louisiana, I was always told, "Use anything and everything that works for you in your rituals".

In considering the astrological associations of stones, consider the moon and rising signs as well. When selecting the stones, choose them for their occult properties. For example, your birthday is March 12, 1952. You are looking for a stone which will enhance your occult powers. In reading our list of stones we see that Jade has the occult properties which are said to enhance one's occult powers. We also see that Jade is a powerful stone for those born in the signs of Virgo, Libra and Aquarius. March 12th is in the sun sign Pisces, but

---

*I use the stones and their occult properties as taught by Al Manning at the E.S.P. Lab. in California.

on this day the moon entered the sign of Libra, the Jade will work equally well even though the sun is in Pisces.

AGATE......................Its astrological associations are Taurus and Gemini. Said to attract peace, victory in games, happiness and good luck. Considered strongest when used by those under the signs of Gemini and Taurus.

AMETHYST..............The astrological associations are Aries and Aquarius. Attracts love, good luck, helps to prevent drunkenness, said to be a protector against evil sorcery. Amethyst is best when used by Aries or Aquarius.

BERYL.......................No astrological associations are attached to this stone. Said to attract deep romance and love. Can bring hope. Also can have protective qualities.

BLOODSTONE.....Scorpio and Pisces are the astrological associations attached to this stone. Bloodstone is also known as Carnelian. It is said to bring friendship, calm angry people and soothe flaring tempers. It is said to be protective against the evil eye and depression. It is strongest when used by those of Virgo, Scorpio and Pisces.

CORAL.....................Associated with Taurus and Sagittarius. Coral is considered one of the strongest protective stones. Protects against the evil eye, all spells intended to harm the wearer, natural disasters and unfortunate occurrences. It is associated with the planet Venus. Coral is said to be especially powerful when used by those with their sun, moon or rising signs in Taurus, Sagittarius or Libra.

DIAMOND...............Its astrological associations are Aries and Leo. Believed to attract power, riches, and friends. Said to be excellent for reconciling differences between those who have quarreled. This stone symbolizes peace, fidelity and opulence. Said to be strongest when used by those of the signs Aries and Leo.

EMERALD...........Associated with Taurus, Gemini and Cancer. A stone with the qualities of precognition and the ability to see into the future. The Emerald nurtures love and beauty, and turns all negative spells back to the sender. When used by those of the signs of Taurus, Gemini and Cancer, it is most powerful.

GARNET ....Aries is its astrological association. This stone attracts purity, sincerity and understanding. Garnet tends to be a bit stuffy and victorian, but can be useful to the signs of Aquarius and Capricorn.

JASPER ....Scorpio is associated with Jasper. It is said that Jasper can protect from pain and guard one's independence. It brings its wearer good fortune and protection from the controlling influences of others. It is best used by the signs of Virgo and Sagittarius.

JADE...................The astrological associations are Virgo, Libra and Aquarius. A stone that has been considered a sacred stone for centuries, bringing good luck, protection from disease or evil spirits. Said to enhance one's occult powers. It presents serenity and immortality. Jade is a powerful stone for those of the signs of Libra, Virgo and Aquarius.

LAPIS...................Sagittarius is this stone's astrological associa-
LAZULI   tion. Said to have the qualities of attracting powerful and highly evolved spirits. It has been believed that the possessor of this

stone was endowed with great supernatural powers. Lapis Lazuli is powerful when used by those with their sun, moon or rising signs in Sagittarius.

MOONSTONE....Its astrological association is Cancer. Said to be a stone of love. It has the qualities of protecting love and inspiring tender passions. It is considered especially powerful when worn by those with the sun, moon or rising sign in Cancer.

OPAL ....Cancer, Libra and Scorpio are the astrological associations. Opal is considered a very dangerous stone to wear for those who are not in tune with it. This stone is mystical by nature and brings good luck and extra mental powers to those of the signs of Libra, Cancer and Scorpio. CAUTION—if you are not of these three signs, please experiment very carefully with opals.

RUBY ....Associated with the astrological signs of Leo and Capricorn. A stone with the qualities of power, loyalty and courage. Ruby is a focuser of occult energy. It protects from trouble, and is an aid in love and passion. Best when used by those with the signs of Cancer, Leo and Capricorn.

SAPPHIRE............Taurus, Virgo, Libra and Aquarius have been associated with Sapphire. Considered a stone of witchcraft and occult powers, it tends to radiate gentleness and peace. This stone is good for bringing justice and truth to light. It is most powerful for those of the signs of Taurus, Virgo, Libra and Aquarius.

SARDONYX.........Its astrological associations are Leo and

Virgo. Has protective qualities against spells and incantations. It tends to strengthen the wits of its wearer and imports warmth and precision. Strongest when used by those of Leo and Virgo.

TOPAZ ....Aries and Scorpio are Topaz's astrological associations. Gives protection to warriors, has the qualities to put demons to flight and vanquishes the evil spells of sorcerers. Topaz has been used for divining purposes to locate water and treasure. This stone is most powerful for those with the signs of Aries, Gemini, Scorpio and Sagittarius.

TURQUOISE........The astrological associations with turquoise are Taurus, Libra and Sagittarius. Believed to bring love and courage. It is said to be a protector against violence in thought and deed. Turquoise is also good for reducing bodily and mental tensions. This stone is best when used by those of the signs of Taurus, Libra and Sagittarius.

ZIRCON ....Taurus and Aquarius are associated with Zircon, a stone which attracts fame and fortune. It is considered to be a wishing stone. It is also a protector against accidents or natural disasters. This stone is strongest for Taurus and Aquarius.

Here are other things which can be used in making a gris-gris bag:

1. Lodestones—if you can buy the big lodestones, you can always break them into smaller pieces with a hammer. This way you get more for your money. Lodestones are usually used in pairs one to attract the positive forces, one to repel the negative.

2. Four leaf clovers—for luck.
3. Small rabbit's foot.
4. Small crosses or a crucifix—to symbolize faith.
5. Coins—in your bag designed to attract riches.
6. Powers—for love, money, gambling luck, uncrossing, etc.
7. Dice—to symbolize the desire to acquire luck or money through this manner.
8. Talismans—which have been made on parchment.
9. Some like to add medals of their patron saint in their bag to symbolize their faith that this saint will help them acquire their desire for which the bag is made.
10. Pieces of colored cloth or feathers to bring in color symbolism to strengthen the desired vibratory influences the gris-gris bag will contain (refer back to the list of colors for their vibratory meanings).
11. Don't forget to add personal items such as hair, nail parings, a photograph, etc. of the person the bag is made for, because this is what will link the energy contained in the bag to the individual.

I've made mention of the gris-gris bag for being anointed with oil. Naturally if your gris-gris bag is designed to bring love—use love oil or attracting oil; for success—use success oil; if the bag is designed for protection—use protection oil, etc. Once again the recipes for making these oils will be given in Part II of this book.

When you anoint the gris-gris bag, apply the appropriate oil to the outer edges of the bag. The anointing must be repeated once a week. Therefore, if you are making a gris-gris bag for another, it will be necessary that you give them a small bottle of the oil and tell them how and when to anoint the bag. It was a very common practice among the voodoo workers during Marie Laveau's time, as well as today, to sell the various oils and other items they may need to their clients. The weekly anointing of the gris-gris bag is always done on the day the bag was made. That is, if you make a gris-gris bag on a Thursday, the bag is anointed again every Thursday afterwards.

Let's begin putting all this together, and then actually make a few gris-gris bags. Feel free to make any changes in the rituals that will blend in your own personality, such as using your own chants or using the herbs which are in harmony with your own personality. It is your own energy giving the power behind the ritual. The more of yourself you put into your work, the stronger it will work for you. To illustrate how to make a gris-gris bag, I'm using my own personal ritual. If you know of another consecration ritual which you prefer, by all means use it.

Chanting is a part of the ritual work. When chanting, always use a low tone of voice. Practice using some of the chants in this book. When the words rattle in your throat and head, you will know that you are doing the chant correctly.

Some practictitioners like to have the person present at the time they are making a gris-gris bag for another. Perhaps you may like to continue this practice; if so, the individual will sit at the right of the altar during the gris-gris bag's construction. Don't forget to keep a pair of scissors near the altar to cut some strands of hair or clip the fingernails of the person you're making the gris-gris bag for.

PROTECT YOUR HOME

Every man's home is his castle. But, in this day and age, it is not practical to build a moat around your home to protect it from intruders and other outside disturbances as was done with the castles of old. Fortunately, this sort of protection is still available to us today. All that is necessary is to build a protective quality into the cleansed aura of your home. Before you proceed in doing this, I would advise you to first thoroughly cleanse your home of all negative vibrations.

Most practitioners will agree that the best time to do any

cleansings on a home or building is during the waning phase of the moon, whereas *protections* should be done during the waxing phase of the moon.

To build your protection, you will need the following:

1. a red flannel or chamois bag
2. a tbsp. of five-finger grass (said to protect against the evil that five fingers can do)
3. a tbsp. of powdered bay leaves
4. a large clove of garlic
5. a piece of mandrake root
6. a small piece of iron (symbolizing strength in your protection)

Items two through five will be put into the gris-gris bag. You will also need as part of your ritual equipment:

7. two white candles
8. one black candle (to signify Saturn's influence over homes, buildings, etc.)
9. one bottle of Protection Oil
10. one bottle of Blessing Oil
11. Circle of Protection Incense

Layout of the altar is as follows:

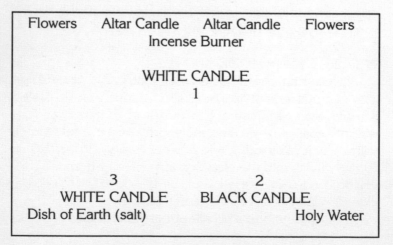

Flowers	Altar Candle	Altar Candle	Flowers
	Incense Burner		

WHITE CANDLE
1

3
WHITE CANDLE
Dish of Earth (salt)

2
BLACK CANDLE
Holy Water

Dress white candle #1 with Blessing Oil.
Dress black candle #2 with Blessing Oil.
Dress white candle #3 with Protection Oil.

1. Do steps one through five as given in the Preliminary to Ritual (page 9). The Psychic/Spiritual Development Herb Candle is put above the Holy Water.
2. Light white candle #1 giving the affirmation:
    > *Here do I light the candle which*
    > *will symbolize__(name)__'s*
    > *sincere desire that his/her*
    > *home will be a fortress,*
    > *keeping away intruders and*
    > *evil influences.*
3. Light black candle #2 while affirming:
    > *Saturn's influence now takes sway,*
    > *to bless this gris-gris in every way.*
    > *A power protection I do say,*
    > *protecting the home where it will lay.*
4. Light white candle #3, again affirming:
    > *Energy white, energy bright;*
    > *strengthening the charm I make this night.*
    > *A powerful protection is your energy,*
    > *as my charm is made lovingly.*
5. Begin filling the gris-gris bag as you chant the following:
    > *Five-finger grass,*
    > *your powers last,*
    > *to protect from harm*
    > *five fingers form.*
    > *At your side your strength*
    > *has a boost,*
    > *from bay leaves, garlic and*
    > *mandrake root.*
    > *Strong as iron you will be,*
    > *to the home where you give your energy.*

Continue this chanting until the bag is filled. Sew or tie the bag to prevent its contents from spilling out.

6. Anoint the gris-gris bag with Protection Oil and lay it in the center of the triangle of candles. Place both hands palms down over the bag as you chant the following:

> *Gris-gris working strong,*
> *all the day and night long.*
> *Protect the home where you lay,*
> *keep all harm and evil at bay.*
> *A strong protection you will be,*
> *to the home that does keep thee.*
> *And thus no harm can penetrate,*
> *the walls your energy permeates.*

Chant three, five, seven or nine times while willing protective energy into the gris-gris bag. Allow the bag to remain within the triangle of lit candles as you do the following:

7. Put some more Circle of Protection Incense in your censor and cense all walls that mark off the outside boundaries of your home or apartment as you chant:

> *These walls may have an aura of their own,*
> *but this incense helps set the tone.*
> *A mighty shield of protection you'll be,*
> *keeping harm from coming near thee.*
> *Your energy works to dispel you see,*
> *robbers, murderers, and harm that be.*
> *Keeping your occupants safe and free,*
> *from outside harm in the world that be.*

If you are an individual who lives in a private home, you should cense the walls outside the home while using your chant. Obviously an apartment dweller may not be able to do this, therefore, it is permissible only to cense the area around your front door.

8. Return to your altar and proceed to consecrate your gris-gris bag. Sprinkle both sides of your gris-gris bag as you affirm:

> *With water do I consecrate this charm*
> *giving a protective aura to the walls*
> *of the house where it is kept.*

Sprinkle both sides of the bag with earth (salt) and affirm:

> *With earth do I consecrate the charm*
> *which will give a protective aura*
> *to the walls in the home where it*
> *is kept.*

Pass both sides of the gris-gris bag through the flames of both white candles and the black candle which affirming:

> *With fire do I consecrate this charm*
> *which will give a protective aura to*
> *the walls in the home where it*
> *is kept.*

Pass both sides of the bag through the incense smoke and affirm:

> *With air do I consecrate this charm*
> *which will give a protective aura*
> *to the walls in the home where*
> *it is kept.*

9. Extinguish your candles in reverse order of lighting them. Hang your protective gris-gris bag above the front door.
10. Close ritual giving thanks for the protection which you will enjoy.

NOTE: When visited in the home by negative people (e. g. those who have negative outlooks on life, full of prejudices, etc.), it is wise to do the following immediately after their visit is over and they are gone. Take a handful of blessed sea salt and throw it out the front door, then proceed to sprinkle your walls and floors with a tea made from basil leaves.

PROTECTION FROM ACCIDENTS/DANGER

You will need the following materials:

1. a red flannel or chamois bag
2. an item belonging to the person who will wear the charm
3. dog rose (an herb)
4. heather
5. comfrey
6. five-finger grass
7. mullein
8. sandalwood
9. one small pair of lodestones

NOTE: Items two through nine will be put into the bag. The pair of lodestones is counted as two items. Aside from your regular altar equipment you will need:

10. one bottle of gardenia oil
    or jasmine oil
11. one white candle
12. one red candle
13. one lt. blue candle

The three candles mentioned above will be placed in the form of a triangle with one point up in the center of your altar. Layout of the altar is as follows:

Flowers	Altar Candle	Altar Candle	Flowers

Incense Burner
WHITE CANDLE
1

LT. BLUE CANDLE   RED CANDLE
3   2

Dish of Earth (sea salt)   Holy Water

Dress white candle #1 with Blessing Oil.
Dress red candle #2 with Blessing Oil.
Dress lt. blue candle #3 with Protection Oil.

1. Perform steps one through five as given in the Preliminary to Ritual (page 9). Your Psychic/Spiritual Development Herb candle is placed above your Holy Water.
2. Light white candle #1 as you affirm:
   > *Let this light symbolize the*
   > *sincere belief that his gris-gris*
   > *will flood __(name)__'s aura*
   > *with a protective quality from*
   > *accidents and danger.*
3. Light red candle #2 while affirming:
   > *The influence of Mars*
   > *lends his blessings here,*
   > *to protect this person*
   > *from enemies near.*
4. Light lt. blue candle #3 and affirm:
   > *Protection that's wanted,*
   > *protection desired.*
   > *This energy flow,*
   > *with the herbs we sew.*
   > *In our protective charm,*
   > *against man's harm.*
5. Begin filling your gris-gris bag as you chant:
   > *Dog rose, heather, comfrey, see,*
   > *protective qualities are with thee.*
   > *Five-finger grass, mullein, too,*
   > *giving aid, protection true.*
   > *Sandalwood and lodestones here,*
   > *help bring protective power near.*

   Continue this chanting until the bag is filled, and sew up or tie the top to prevent the gris-gris from spilling out.
6. Anoint the gris-gris bag with Gardenia or Jasmine Oil

and lay the bag in the center of the triangle. Place both hands palms down over the bag as you chant the following:

> *Charm of protection that I build,*
> *I know that you will fit the bill.*
> *To this person's aura, see,*
> *you'll give your protective energy.*
> *Protect from harm of man or beast,*
> *encountered accidents the least.*
> *An aura pure, white and bright,*
> *sends all harm at sight to flight.*
> *Protect from harm of man or beast,*
> *encountered accidents the least.*

Continue the chanting three, five, seven or nine times.

7. When through chanting, begin to consecrate your gris-gris bag. Sprinkle both sides of the gris-gris bag with Holy Water as you affirm:

> *With water do I consecrate this charm,*
> *a storehouse of energy to protect its*
> *wearer from accident and harm.*

Sprinkle both sides of the bag with earth (sea salt); again affirm:

> *With earth do I consecrate this charm,*
> *a storehouse of energy to protect its*
> *wearer from accident and harm.*

Pass both sides of the gris-gris bag through the flames of the white, red, and lt. blue candle while affirming:

> *With fire do I consecrate this charm,*
> *a storehouse of energy to protect its*
> *wearer from accident and harm.*

Pass both sides of the bag through the incense smoke as you affirm:

> *With air do I consecrate this charm,*
> *a storehouse of energy to protect its*
> *wearer from accident and harm.*

8. Place the gris-gris bag back in the center of the triangle, and allow the candles to burn for the remainder of the hour. Extinguish the candles in the reverse order of lighting them. Close the ritual.

STOPPING GOSSIP

Materials needed:

1. a red flannel or chamois bag
2. a piece of cloth to which you have drawn in ink the image of a human face.
3. an item of hair or clothing belonging to the person who will wear the bag.
4. a piece of John the Conqueror root
5. a tbsp. of slippery elm
6. a half tsp. of gag root
7. a needle and black thread

Items two through five will be put into your bag. You will also need the following:

8. two white candles
9. one red candle
10. Gris Gris Faible Incense

The three candles mentioned above will be placed in the center of your altar in the form of a triangle with one point up. Layout of the altar is as follows:

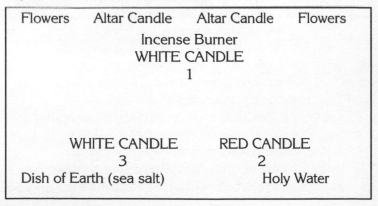

Flowers	Altar Candle	Altar Candle	Flowers
	Incense Burner		
	WHITE CANDLE		
	1		
	WHITE CANDLE	RED CANDLE	
	3	2	
Dish of Earth (sea salt)		Holy Water	

White candle #1 is dressed with Blessing Oil.
Red candle #2 is dressed with Success Oil.
White candle #3 is dressed with Power Oil.

1. Perform steps one through five as given in the Pre-liminary to Ritual. Your Psychic/Spiritual Development Herb Candle is placed above the Holy Water.
2. Taking your black thread and needle, begin to sew the mouth shut on the face you have drawn on your piece of cloth. Here the color black is being used to symbolize the fact that we are putting a stop to vicious rumors, gossip; NOT to cause any harm or injury to another. Chant as you sew:
    The mouth I bind this very day,
    binds fast the evil mouths can say.
    Nevermore causing distress and alarm,
    nevermore able to cause harm.
3. Light white candle #1 as you affirm the following:
    The fire of truth and sincerity burns,
    ____(name)____'s faith in this charm
    will never turn. As his/her faith is
    steadfast and true.
4. Light red candle #2 while affirming:
    A blessing comes this way today,
    an influence of Mars all will say.
    To overthrow the enemies that be,
    who seek to harm through gossip see.
5. Light white candle #3 again affirming:
    Truth and justice enters here,
    a quality many hold so dear.
    To counteract the many lies,
    in the minds where, slander,
    gossip, resides.
6. Place the image on which you have sewn the mouth shut in your gris-gris bag and proceed to fill the bag with

the rest of your materials as you chant (Note: If you like, you can tie the personal item of the individual, be it strands of hair or clothing, to the John the Conqueror root before placing this item in your bag):

> *Vanishing foes you will see,*
> *Johnny the Conqueror is with thee.*
> *Slippery elm and gag root,*
> *help shut the mouths evil words shoot.*
> *No longer gossip can harm thee,*
> *beginning this day you will see.*

Extinguish the candles in reverse order of their lighting. Close ritual.

NOTE: If you like, you can give a word of advice to the person you have made the gris-gris bag for. These should be words which are encouraging and helpful, for example: "As you wear this charm, live your life with honesty, care and concern for others, but use wisdom and don't meddle in the affairs of others, and don't go back on your word when it has been given." As you can see, this can be done for any charm you make for another to wear, simply by using words of advice in respect to the nature of the gris-gris bag.

MAINTAINING GOOD HEALTH
To make this gris-gris bag you will need the following:
1. a red flannel or chamois bag
2. a personal item belonging to the individual wearing the bag
3. rosemary
4. carnation
5. eucalyptus
6. gotu kola
7. a bottle of Health Attracting Oil
8. one white candle
9. one red candle

10. one purple candle

Items two through six will be put into the gris-gris bag. Layout of the altar is as follows:

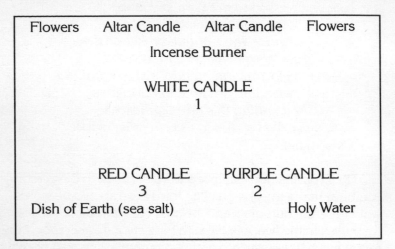

Flowers   Altar Candle   Altar Candle   Flowers

Incense Burner

WHITE CANDLE
1

RED CANDLE   PURPLE CANDLE
3   2
Dish of Earth (sea salt)   Holy Water

The white candle is dressed with Blessing Oil.
The purple candle is dressed with Blessing Oil.
The red candle is dressed with Health Attracting Oil.

1. Perform steps one through five as given in the Preliminary to Ritual. The Psychic/Spiritual Herb Candle is placed above the Holy Water.
2. Light white candle #1 as you give the following affirmation:

> *This flame does burn to symbolize*
> *the sincere belief that ___(name)___*
> *can have and maintain good health.*
> *Through this faith will the desire*
> *be realized.*

3. Light purple candle #2 while affirming:

> *Mercury, since days of old,*
> *matters of health you hold.*

> *Your blessing now we seek this day,*
> *as healing energy is sent this way.*

4. Light red candle #3 as you affirm:

> *Positive energy,*
> *vigorous it will be,*
> *restoring health and strength you see,*
> *captured in this charm to be.*

5. Begin putting your ingredients into your bag as you chant:

> *Rosemary, we are told*
> *of your power a memory to hold.*
> *Working here, eucalyptus,*
> *against colds which try to grab us.*
> *Gotu Kola and carnation,*
> *helps to maintain a*
> *strong constitution.*

6. When the bag is filled, sew or tie the top to keep the contents from spilling out. Anoint the gris-gris bag with Health Attracting Oil and lay it in the center of the triangle of burning candles. Place both hands palms down over your charm and will your energy to flow as you chant:

> *Though you have no money,*
> *you do have wealth.*
> *For you now have,*
> *your excellent health.*
> *To have, to hold,*
> *forever more,*
> *vigor and strength,*
> *you have in store.*
> *Though you have no money,*
> *you do have wealth.*
> *For you now have,*
> *excellent health.*

Continue chanting for three, five, seven or nine times.

7. When you feel that you have given enough energy to the

gris-gris bag, consecrate it in the following manner by sprinkling both sides of the charm with Holy Water as you affirm:

> *With water do I consecrate this*
> *gris-gris, a storehouse of energy*
> *conducive to maintaining*
> *good health.*

Sprinkle both sides of the charm with earth (sea salt), again affirming:

> *With earth do I consecrate this*
> *charm, a storehouse of energy con-*
> *ducive to maintaining good health.*

Pass both sides of the gris-gris bag through the flames of all three candles as you affirm:

> *With fire do I consecrate this*
> *charm, a storehouse of energy con-*
> *ducive to maintaining good health.*

Pass both sides of the charm through the incense smoke while affirming:

> *With air do I consecrate this charm,*
> *a storehouse of energy conducive*
> *to maintaining good health.*

8. Replace the gris-gris bag in the center of the triangle and allow the candles to burn for the remainder of the hour. Extinguish the candles in reverse order of their lighting. Close ritual.

TO INCREASE LOVE IN YOUR LIFE

You will need the following materials:

1. a red flannel or chamois bag
2. one pair of lodestones
3. one small piece of orris root
4. 1 tsp. of passion flower
5. 1 tsp. love drawing powder
6. 1 beryl (this is a stone)

7. 1 tsp. vervian
8. 1 tsp. lavender
9. a personal item belonging to the individual

Items two through nine will be put into the gris-gris bag. The pair of lodestones is considered as two items, giving us nine separate items used in the bag.

Aside from your regular altar equipment you will need:

10. 1 white candle
11. 1 pink candle
12. 1 green candle
13. 1 bottle of love oil
14. Enticing Love Incense

The three candles mentioned above will be placed in the form of a triangle. All ingredients used to make the gris-gris bag will be placed in the center of this triangle.

The layout of the altar for this ritual is as follows:

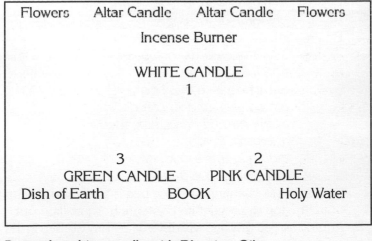

Flowers	Altar Candle	Altar Candle	Flowers
	Incense Burner		
	WHITE CANDLE		
	1		
	3	2	
	GREEN CANDLE	PINK CANDLE	
Dish of Earth	BOOK		Holy Water

Dress the white candle with Blessing Oil.
Dress the pink candle with Love Oil.

Dress the green candle with Blessing Oil.

1. Light the white candle giving the affirmation:
   > Here do I light the candle symbolizing
   > the endless sincerity and faith which
   > ____(name)____ has in mind, body
   > and soul. The sincere belief is that
   > this gris-gris will help increase love
   > in his/her life from this day forth.

2. Light the pink candle affirming:
   > Symbolized in this candle is the
   > quality of love which will be imbued
   > in this charm of love. As this candle
   > burns, this love is strengthened. As
   > love is given, so will it return.

3. Light the green candle while affirming:
   > Venus' influence is symbolized here.
   > This candle burns giving added
   > strength, a constant flow of energy
   > to help continually energize this
   > gris-gris for its wearer.

4. Begin filling the gris-gris bag as you chant:
   > Lodestones, orris root, passion flower
   > and love powder,
   > attracting love this hour,
   > which I know you can do.
   > Stone named beryl, lavender,
   > and vervain too,
   > aiding in this work I do,
   > increasing love that's true.

   Continue this chanting until the bag is filled, and sew up
   or tie the top to prevent its contents from spilling out.

5. Anoint the gris-gris bag with love oil and lay the bag in the
   center of the triangle. Place both hands palms down over
   the bag as you chant the following:

Charm of love, made by me,
filling with energy.
To bring that which is good,
bringing love as you should.
Each day, this charm is worn
its power of love is felt, that's warm.
The power grows in strength each day,
Bringing love its wearer's way.

Keep up the chanting three, five, seven or nine times until you feel that the gris-gris bag is embued with enough energy.

6. Now comes the consecration of the gris-gris bag. Sprinkle both sides of the gris-gris bag with Holy Water, using the following:

With water do I consecrate this charm,
an instrument bringing forth love.

Sprinkle both sides of the gris-gris bag with earth, saying:

With earth do I consecrate this charm,
an instrument to bring its wearer love.

Pass both sides of the gris-gris bag through the flames of the white, pink and green candle while affirming:

With fire do I consecrate this charm,
an instrument bringing forth love.

Pass both sides of the gris-gris bag through the incense smoke while saying:

With air do I consecrate this charm,
an instrument to bring its wearer love.

7. Place the gris-gris bag back in the center of the triangle. Allow the candles to burn for the remainder of the hour. Extinguish the candles in the reverse order of lighting them.

8. Close the ritual.

TO WIN THE LOVE OF ANOTHER

NOTE: Since this ritual is designed for love that is both of an emotional and physical nature, it is a good idea to use herbs associated with love and passion.

You will need the following materials:

1. a red flannel or chamois bag
2. a personal item from both parties the gris-gris is to inspire love between
3. a symbol such as a heart made from red wax to which you can attach the personal items belonging to both people involved
4. 1 tsp. cubeb berries
5. 1 small piece of orris root
6. 1 tsp. spikenard herb
7. 1 tsp. cloves
8. 1 tsp. damiana
9. 1 tsp. juniper berries

Items two through nine will be put into the gris-gris bag. Once again we will be using nine different items for this ritual.

Besides your regular altar equipment, you will need the following:

10. 1 white candle
11. 1 red candle
12. 1 green candle
13. 1 bottle of Love Oil or Seduction Oil
14. Enticing Love Incense
15. 1 bottle of Blessing Oil

Layout of the altar is on following page:

Dress the white candle with Blessing Oil.
Dress the red candle with Love Oil or Seduction Oil.
Dress the green candle with Blessing Oil.

1. Light the white candle and affirm:
   Here do I light the candle symbolizing

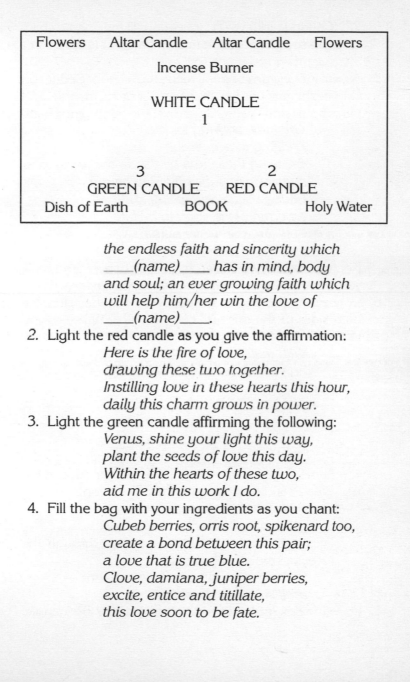

| Flowers | Altar Candle | Altar Candle | Flowers |

Incense Burner

WHITE CANDLE
1

3   **2**
GREEN CANDLE   **RED CANDLE**
Dish of Earth   **BOOK**   Holy Water

> *the endless faith and sincerity which*
> *____(name)____ has in mind, body*
> *and soul; an ever growing faith which*
> *will help him/her win the love of*
> *____(name)____.*

2. Light the red candle as you give the affirmation:
> *Here is the fire of love,*
> *drawing these two together.*
> *Instilling love in these hearts this hour,*
> *daily this charm grows in power.*

3. Light the green candle affirming the following:
> *Venus, shine your light this way,*
> *plant the seeds of love this day.*
> *Within the hearts of these two,*
> *aid me in this work I do.*

4. Fill the bag with your ingredients as you chant:
> *Cubeb berries, orris root, spikenard too,*
> *create a bond between this pair;*
> *a love that is true blue.*
> *Clove, damiana, juniper berries,*
> *excite, entice and titillate,*
> *this love soon to be fate.*

Continue with the chant as you fill the gris-gris bag, and sew up or tie the top so that the ingredients of the gris-gris will not spill out.

5. Anoint the gris-gris bag with either Love Oil or Seduction Oil. Lay the gris-gris bag in the center of the triangle, and place both hands palms down over the bag as you chant:

> Gris-gris working for me,
> creating love energy.
> Bringing these two hearts as one,
> this growing love has now begun.
> Entice, excite and titillate,
> a burning love soon to be fate.
> Fulfilling the desire within,
> as this love affair begins.

Keep up the chanting three, five, seven or nine times until you feel the charm is imbued with sufficient power.

6. Consecrate the bag in the following manner: sprinkle both sides of the gris-gris bag with Holy Water as you affirm:

> With water do I consecrate this gris-gris,
> an instrument inspiring love.

Sprinkle both sides of the gris-gris bag with earth as you affirm:

> With earth do I consecrate this charm,
> an instrument inspiring love.

Pass both sides of the gris-gris bag through the flames of the white candle, the red candle and the green candle as you give the affirmation:

> With fire do I consecrate this gris-
> gris, an instrument inspiring love.

Pass both sides of the gris-gris bag through the incense smoke as you affirm:

> With air do I consecrate this charm,
> an instrument inspiring love.

7. Place the gris-gris bag back in the center of the triangle.

Allow the candles to burn for the remainder of the hour. Extinquish them in reverse order of lighting them.
8. Close the ritual.

TO BE MORE SEDUCTIVE

NOTE: If you want to be more seductive to women, then you will need something to symbolize the vagina (a stone or rock with a natural hole through it, as an example). If you want to be more seductive to men, you will need something to represent the penis (round oblong shells found on the beach, another example). Of course, change the words to fit the desire. This ritual is designed to increase your own sexual encounters.

You will need the following materials:
1. a red flannel or chamois bag
2. a personal item belonging to the individual
3. a small piece of red cloth or a red feather
4. 1 tsp. of Canada snake root
5. 1 tsp. of damiana
6. 1 tsp. dill seed.

Items two through six are to be put into the bag. In this ritual we will use five ingredients.

Besides your regular altar equipment you will need the following:
7. 1 white candle
8. 1 red candle
9. 1 green candle
10. 1 bottle of Seduction Oil
11. Enticing Love Incense
12. 1 bottle of Blessing Oil

NOTE: The altar will be laid out in the same manner used for making the gris-gris bag "To Win the Love of Another". Since you will be using the same candles in this ritual, refer to that diagram (page 60).

Dress the white candle with Blessing Oil.
Dress the red candle with Seduction Oil.
Dress the green candle with Blessing Oil.

1. Light the white candle giving the affirmation:
   > *Symbolized here is the growing faith*
   > *and sincerity which ____(name)____ has*
   > *in this gris-gris to help bring its*
   > *wearer a potent, seductive aura.*
2. Light the red candle while you give the affirmation:
   > *Here is needed energy,*
   > *increasing sexuality.*
   > *You are seductive, all will say,*
   > *as this energy comes your way.*
3. Light the green candle as you affirm:
   > *Venus gives an influence here,*
   > *to bless this charm held so dear.*
   > *A constant flow of energy,*
   > *increasing seductibility.*
4. Begin filling the gris-gris bag as you chant the following:
   > *Canada snake root, work for me,*
   > *damiana and dill seed,*
   > *lend to me the help I need.*
   > *Red the color of desire,*
   > *working now within this hour.*
   > *Increasing my seductibility,*
   > *for I am sexy, all can see.*
5. Anoint the gris-gris bag with your seduction oil. Lay the gris-gris bag in the center of the triangle. Place both hands palms down over the bag as you chant:
   > *The power of seduction,*
   > *working for me,*
   > *increasing, strengthening, steadily.*

> *Enticing others to desire me,*
> *into my arms, they fly readily.*
> *A night of sex, a night of bliss,*
> *for my lips they long to kiss.*
> *And with a smile, they walk away,*
> *eager to return another day.*

Continue the chanting three, five, seven or nine times until you feel that the gris-gris bag has absorbed enough energy.

6. Consecrate the gris-gris bag as follows: sprinkle the gris-gris bag on both sides with Holy Water as you affirm:

> *With water do I consecrate this charm,*
> *an instrument aiding its wearer to be*
> *seductive.*

Sprinkle both sides of the gris-gris bag with earth as you give the affirmation:

> *With earth do I consecrate this charm,*
> *an instrument aiding its wearer to be*
> *seductive.*

Pass both sides of the gris-gris bag through the flames of the white candle, the red candle and the green candle as you affirm the following:

> *With fire do I consecrate this charm,*
> *an instrument aiding its wearer to be*
> *seductive.*

Pass both sides of the gris-gris bag through the incense smoke as you affirm:

> *With air do I consecrate this charm,*
> *an instrument aiding its wearer to be*
> *seductive.*

7. Place the gris-gris bag back in the center of the triangle. Allow the candles to burn for the remainder of the hour. Extinguish them in reverse order to lighting them.

8. Close ritual.

NOTE: It is not uncommon to use such personal items as semen for a male, and menstrual blood for a woman in this sort of ritual.

TO OBTAIN MONEY

You will need the following materials:

1. a red flannel or chamois bag
2. a piece of counterfeit coin or real money
3. 1 small pair of lodestones
4. 1 buckeye
5. 1 tbsp. of five-finger grass
6. 1 tsp. of Money Drawing Powder
7. 1 tsp. of silver weed

Items two through seven will be put into the gris-gris bag itself. In this ritual we will be working with seven different items.

You will also need the following:

8. 1 bottle of Money Drawing Oil
9. 1 white candle
10. 1 yellow candle (using the Sun's influence in this rite)
11. 1 green candle
12. Shower of Gold Incense

Arrange the altar as follows:

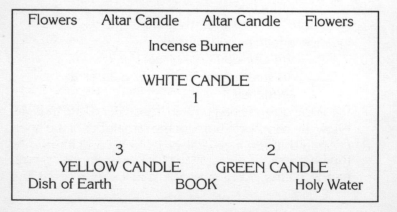

Flowers	Altar Candle	Altar Candle	Flowers
	Incense Burner		
	WHITE CANDLE 1		
3 YELLOW CANDLE		2 GREEN CANDLE	
Dish of Earth	BOOK		Holy Water

Dress the white candle with Blessing Oil.
Dress the green candle with Money Drawing Oil.
Dress the yellow candle with Blessing Oil.

1. Light the white candle while giving the affirmation:
    > *This candle symbolizes the ever-*
    > *growing faith and sincerity which*
    > *____(name)____ has, that through the*
    > *help of this gris-gris bag he/she*
    > *will have money in his/her life.*
2. Light the green candle as you affirm:
    > *Here is the money which is deserved,*
    > *coming this way as my words are heard.*
    > *A constant flow of cash you see,*
    > *in his/her hands it will be.*
3. Light the yellow candle as you give the following affirmation:
    > *Added strength comes from the sun.*
    > *as this work has now begun.*
    > *To make this charm for money*
    > *giving constant energy.*
4. Begin to fill the gris-gris bag with your ingredients as you chant:
    > *The lodestones attract to me,*
    > *money which I see.*
    > *Buckeye, five-finger grass,*
    > *giving aid which will last.*
    > *money drawing powder,*
    > *and silver weed,*
    > *Bringing to me money, which I need.*

    Keep up the chanting until the bag is filled and sew up the top or tie it to prevent the contents from spilling out.
5. Anoint the gris-gris bag with your money drawing oil. Lay the bag down in the center of the triangle, place both hands palms down over the bag as you chant the

following:

> Money flowing directly to me,
> in my hands it will be.
> Financial worries, I do not store,
> fulfilled my needs forevermore.
> My charm for money working for me,
> to bring me money constantly.
> My financial needs will be fulfilled,
> beginning this day as I have willed.

Continue the chanting three, five, seven or nine times until you feel the gris-gris bag is filled with enough energy.

6. Consecrate the gris-gris bag as follows: sprinkle both sides of the gris-gris bag with Holy Water as you give the affirmation:

> With water do I consecrate this charm,
> an instrument to continually attract
> money.

Sprinkle both sides of the gris-gris bag with earth as you affirm:

> With earth do I consecrate this charm,
> an instrument to continually attract
> money.

Pass both sides of the gris-gris bag through the flames of the white candle, green candle and yellow candle as you affirm:

> With fire do I consecrate this charm,
> an instrument to continually attract
> money.

Pass both sides of the gris-gris bag through the incense smoke as you give the affirmation:

> With air do I consecrate this charm,
> an instrument to continually attract
> money.

7. Place the gris-gris bag in the center of the triangle.

Allow the candles to burn for the remainder of the hour. Extinguish the candles in reverse order of lighting them.
8. Close ritual.

After The Ritual

After the candles have been extinguished, the gris-gris bag will be ready to give to the person to wear. The energy contained within the gris-gris bag is strongest when worn next to the skin. If you want to make a gris-gris bag which will have an effect on another, such as to keep a loved one faithful, and you do not want them to know about it (which is best in this case), it is no great problem. Simply hide the gris-gris bag under the cushion or behind their favorite chair, under their side of the mattress or taped in back of the headboard on their side of the bed; it can be placed under the front steps in which the individual would pass over it as they enter or leave the house, etc. The gris-gris bag doesn't have to be worn, but it must come within reach of the person's aura periodically during the day if it is to have any effect on them whatsoever. Some practitioners, for cursing purposes, will hang the gris-gris from a tree or bush near the victim's front or back door. Every time the victim passes by the tree or bush, his aura will pick up the negative energy transmitted through the gris-gris bag. This is usually referred to as laying the trick.

If for some reason you are not going to wear your gris-gris bag, it should be kept in a small wooden box.

For step five, in the detailed rituals previously given, you will be doing several things at one time:
1. By placing the palms of both hands over the gris-gris bag once it is filled, you should will your energy to flow. Here you are charging or giving extra energy to intensify the aura of the herbs, stones, etc. which are being used to make the gris-gris bag. It is a known fact that humans as well as plant and inanimate objects have an aura of

their own.

2. The use of words, i.e. your chant, defines how this energy is to work for you.

3. As you are using your chant, at this point you should see the desire happening in your mind. The use of words and pictures simultaneously can be very impressive on the subconscious mind.

Over the years much Catholicism has been added to the magick practices in southern Louisiana. I purposely stripped away this influence, but remained true in the procedure used to make a gris-gris bag by chanting as you fill the bag and using chant to charge the bag as in step five, because I felt that the Catholic influence limited the full expression of the individual's personality in making magick.

I believe that the rituals given should give you the idea as to how to make a gris-gris bag for yourself or another. With a little imagination and the information in this book, you should easily be able to construct a gris-gris bag. Don't be afraid to express yourself in your magick, and your ritual will become what they should be—personal rituals.

Chapter Three

DOLLS AND MAGICK

Since ages past, dolls in male and female form have been used in magickal practice in the Old World and by some of the American Indian tribes in the New World. The doll itself is made through ritual and is used as a psychic link between the person and the actual ritual. Contrary to popular belief, the doll does not have to look exactly like the person it represents. However, it is necessary that the person making the doll has a clear mental picture of the person the doll will represent during the doll's construction from start to finish.

In Louisiana, the dolls are made of two basic materials; cloth and clay. The cloth doll is a simple human outline cut from two pieces of material. A hole is left at the top so that the doll can be stuffed. The material used for stuffing the doll can be anything from cotton to straw, Spanish moss to various herbs. Of course, as many items as you can get from the individual the doll represents, without them knowing it, should be mixed with the stuffing material. A cloth doll made to represent a person with red hair and green eyes will have red wool or thread for the hair and the eyes will be sewn on with green thread.

NOTE: Traditionally, the material used to make a cloth doll is

taken from an article of soiled clothing which was worn by the individual the cloth doll will represent.

The clay doll, which is most widely used, will have the basic male or female shaped body. There is a belief about the clay to use in making the doll has been handed down: the clay must come from the mud chimney of a crayfish hole. As with the cloth doll, mix as many items as you can obtain from the individual with the clay as you make the doll.

When both types of dolls are completed, they should be wrapped in clean white linen until the dolls are ready for use in the ritual.

Making a doll to represent another or yourself without some sort of ritual is a useless and harmless act. It is the ritual which impresses itself upon the mind of the operator and strengthens the link between the individual, the will of the operator and the ritual that will affect the individual represented by the doll.

For the doll consecration ritual, the layout of the altar should be done in the following manner:

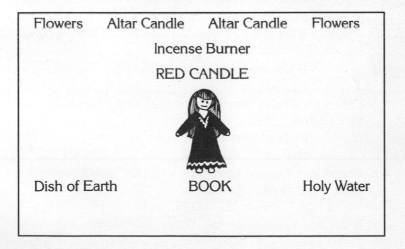

Flowers	Altar Candle	Altar Candle	Flowers
	Incense Burner		
	RED CANDLE		
Dish of Earth	BOOK		Holy Water

1. Light Altar Candles #1 and 2.
2. Light incense; use aura of Enchantment Incense here.
3. Bless the items you are using to make your doll, be it clay or cloth, and proceed to make the doll. Get a clear mental image of the person your doll will represent; hold this mental image in your mind as you concentrate on the person while you are making the doll. To reinforce your concentration keep repeating the following affirmation:

   _____(name)_____, as you I see,
   _____(name)_____, you represent to me.

   Continue this chanting and visualization until the doll is completed. Lay the doll on the altar below the red candle. Place both hands over the doll and will your energy to flow as you chant three, five, seven or nine times:

   Though separate you are,
   you are linked as one.
   As _____(name)_____,
   your life has begun.

4. Pass both sides of the finished doll through the flame of the red candle (the color of blood, the life force), saying:

   With fire do I consecrate
   this doll as _____(name)_____.

   Sprinkle both sides of the doll with Holy Water as you say:

   With water do I consecrate this
   doll as _____(name)_____.

   Pass both sides of the doll through the incense smoke as you affirm:

   With air do I consecrate this
   doll as _____(name)_____.

5. Keep the doll wrapped in clean white linen until it is ready to be used in your ritual.

It has been said that magick and voodoo have no real power, and if you do not believe in these so-called superstitious practices, no one can influence your life for good or evil with the use of magick. In order for the magick to work, as you must be made aware that some sort of magick is being used against you. In a sense, this is somewhat but not altogether true. As it was explained to me by an old Negro Voodoo worker, "You don't have to believe in gris-gris" (a word used to mean anything dealing with magick or voodoo practice in Louisiana). "Now, if the person who practices such things believes in it strong enough, that is all the belief necessary in order to make it work. In fact, you don't have to know at all that someone is working gris-gris against you or for you. It will work as long as the person who practices it believes.

Innate in every human being is a natural form of protection from negativity and evil. This is known as the aura. By attuning yourself to the cosmic white light, you automatically cleanse and give added strength to the aura. A clean and strong aura will protect you, and even send back to the one wishing to harm you the evil sent your way.* The protective power of the aura can also be strengthened by wearing a gris-gris bag designed to protect you from evil. The power of suggestion is strong and does work upon the mind. But, if you know someone is trying to work magick to harm you, you can protect yourself and send back the evil to its sender. People who live their daily lives ignorant of magick and the protective value of the aura are the ones most vulnerable to the evil side of magickal practices. Eventually the so-called black magician will succeed in getting through the protective shield of the aura. These are the ones who almost always do not consider getting help until it is too late, and it becomes difficult to remove the negative condition from their lives. It is for this reason I caution you: *Beware of the silent curse, it can be the most dangerous.*

Many people want to learn magick with the misconcep-

---

*Read more about this in *Psychic Self-Defense and Well-Being* by Denning & Phillips (Llewellyn).

tion that they will no longer have any problems in their lives. Their every wish will be handed to them on a silver platter. This thought about magick belongs to the dream world of television and fiction. We will always have problems, we will always have setbacks in our lives. It is through our problems that we can learn. Our setbacks can help to teach us patience. The use of magick does help in the sense that it can shorten the duration of our prolems, or completely change the course a person's life will take. Yes, magick can even bring our desires into reality. Usually most of our problems are brought upon our own selves as a result of our own thoughtless and foolish actions.

There will be times when your spells will fail. There can be one of many reasons for your failure. Perhaps the very thing that you desire will not be to your benefit. Perhaps you've done a ritual to win the love of another, but during the ritual you did not truly believe within yourself that you would win this person's love. This doubt during the ritual was a silent prayer for failure, and doing the ritual was actually a waste of time and energy in spite of the fact that you were working for something positive. Perhaps you need to spend some more time in developing concentration and creative visualization.

If you are going to do the following rituals for another instead of yourself, try to get the other person to work along with you. In this case they must follow certain instructions. During the time you are working on a ritual for another, they should do the following daily. Burn a special herb candle (these candles you will need to make yourself). Have the person repeat an affirmation as they light the candle, or to ease their mind that they are not doing something evil, they can recite a psalm from the Bible as they burn their candle. Plus, they should take a daily ritual bath to which a tablespoon of Blessed Salt and certain anointing oils have been added to the bath water while the candle is burning.

These special herb candles are made by either mixing in the herb with the wax while making the candle, or by rolling the dressed candle in the powdered herb. You may also sprinkle the herb in the oil and then dress the candle with the oil. Here are some herbs to use:

LOVE...............................Add powdered vervain and powdered passion flower to a red candle or a pink candle, depending on the color you prefer.

PASSION ....Add powdered myrtle and powdered cloves to a red candle.

MARRIAGE.....................Add powdered orange blossoms, powdered orris root and powdered anise seed to a red candle.

HEALING ....Add powdered blessed thistle to a light blue candle.

UNCROSSING...............Add powdered wood betony to a white candle.

CURSING........................Add powdered knot grass to a black candle.

SPIRITUAL AND ....Add powdered anise seed to a purple
PSYCHIC POWER   or white candle, depending on the color you prefer.

LUCK................................Add powdered peony and powdered five-finger grass to a green candle.

PROTECTION...............Add powdered five-finger grass and
FROM EVIL   powdered sandalwood to a light blue candle.

MONEY............................Add powdered thyme, powdered clover and powdered bayberry herb to a green candle.

STOPPING......................Add powdered slippery elm to a white
GOSSIP   candle.

CONFUSING AN..........Add powdered yohimbe root to a
ENEMY   brown candle.

UNDERSTANDING......Add powdered frankincense to a light blue candle.

SUCCESS ....Add powdered cinnamon, powdered Irish moss and powdered five-finger grass to an orange candle.

Of course, these special herb candles will have to be blessed, the ritual objective inscribed on the candle, and the candle dressed with the appropriate oil before it is given to the person to burn. It is best to wrap the candle in white paper cut in the form of a triangle, until the person is ready to burn the candle in their home.

In the rituals that follow, we will be working with dolls, candles, incense and anointing oils. The doll is commonly associated with the practice of magick, but not too many people ever write about using dolls in magick. If you are turned on to the idea of using dolls in your magick, the following rituals will show you an easy way of using dolls in connection with candle burning.

TO ENCOURAGE MARRIAGE
This ritual is best begun on a Friday during the waxing phase of the moon.
Materials needed:

1. 2 cloth dolls—representing both the bride and groom to be.
2. 7 red marriage herb candles dressed with Stray No More Oil
3. 2 orange candles dressed with Courage Oil
4. a sprinkling mixture of two parts Love Drawing Powder and one part Orange Blossoms

5. Enticing Love Incense
6. a 21" length of red ribbon
7. a piece of white linen

NOTE: In this ritual it would be appropriate to dress the dolls as a bride and groom.

Layout of the Altar is as follows:

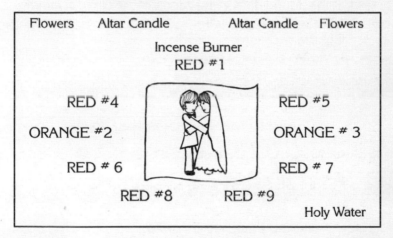

| Flowers | Altar Candle | | Altar Candle | Flowers |

Incense Burner
RED #1

RED #4   RED #5

ORANGE #2   ORANGE # 3

RED # 6   RED # 7

RED #8   RED #9

Holy Water

1. Perform steps one through five as given in the Preliminary to Ritual. The Psychic and Spiritual Development Herb Candle should be placed above the Holy Water.
2. Using the red ribbon, tie the hands of each doll around the back of the other. With the remaining ribbon, wrap it around the waists of both dolls like a belt, tying them together as you chant:
> *Your relationship now,*
> *takes a new turn.*
> *Thoughts of marriage,*
> *in your minds burn.*

> ____(name of bride to be)____ ,
> and ____(name of groom to be)____ ,
> *your wedding day,*
> *you long to see.*
> *Your wedding day,*
> *you seek eagerly.*
> *Your wedding vows you will take,*
> *to be together,*
> *sealing your fate.*

Lay the bound dolls in the center of the circle of candles on the white linen square.

3. Light the red marriage candle #1 as you say:

> *A wedding will be,*
> *between these two,*
> ____(name)____ and ____(name) ____,
> *their love is true.*
> *As their wedding vows, they do take,*
> *to be as one,*
> *their new fate.*

4. Light orange candle #2 as you say:

> *Encouragement comes to thee,*
> ____(name groom)____ ,
> *Your friends and family,*
> *want to see,*
> *you married to,*
> ____(name bride)____
> *happily.*

5. Light orange candle #3 as you say:

> *Encouragement comes to thee,*
> ____(name bride)____ ,
> *Your friends and family,*
> *want to see,*
> *you married to,*
> ____(name groom)____
> *happily.*

6. Sprinkle some of your sprinkling mixture over the dolls as you chant:

> *Your relationship now,*
> *takes a new turn.*
> *Thoughts of marriage,*
> *in your mind burn.*
> *____(name of groom to be)____ ,*
> *your wedding day,*
> *you long to see.*
> *Your wedding day,*
> *you seek eagerly.*
> *Your wedding vows you will take,*
> *to be together,*
> *sealing your fate.*

7. Allow the candles to burn a few minutes as you picture in your mind the couple exchanging their wedding vows and placing the wedding rings on each other's finger.

8. Extinguish the candles in reverse order of lighting them. Repeat each Friday, lighting red candle #1 and #4. On the third Friday, light red candles #1, #4 and #5 and so forth.

9. On the last day of doing the ritual, the dolls are wrapped in the white linen and given to the person who requested the ritual to keep in a safe place.

TO STOP ANOTHER'S INTERFERENCE

This type of ritual is designed to prevent or stop another from interfering with another person or getting involved in a situation.

Materials needed:

1. a cloth doll—representing the person to be stopped
2. one gray candle dressed with Power Oil
3. a sprinkling mixture of equal parts; asafoetida,

calamus root, and graveyard dirt
4. Use either Gris-Gris Faible or Bon Voyage Incense

NOTE: On a piece of paper write, "___(name)___ has stopped interfering completely with ___(name of person or situation)___", or something to this effect. This ritual can also be used to prevent another from gossiping or telling any secrets. In this case the mouth of the doll is sewn up and you add slippery elm to the sprinkling mixture.

Here use the basic altar layout. Do steps one through five.

6. At the altar tie the doll's hands behind its back. Having done this, stand the doll in a corner of the room with its back to the corner.
7. Place the gray candle with your piece of paper under it directly in front of the doll. Light the candle, repeating exactly what you have written on the paper.
8. Use the following chant as you sprinkle some of the mixture over the doll:

> *Your back is to the corner,*
> *your hands are tied.*
> *So you can't help,*
> *but to stand aside.*
> *___(name of person to be stopped)___ ,*
> *you no longer interfere,*
> *with___(name of person or situation)___*
> *mentioned here.*
> *There's nothing more,*
> *you can say or do,*
> *nor have any influence too.*
> *Your actions come to a dead halt,*
> *no longer giving,*
> *the matter (or person) thought.*

9. Allow the candle to burn a few moments as you picture in

your mind that the person has stopped interfering, gossiping, getting involved. As long as the doll is not disturbed or removed from the corner, the person will not be able to interfere, gossip, or whatever. Continue burning the candle daily until it is consumed. NOTE: Some practitioners will use a black candle instead of a gray candle for this type of ritual.

THE JUVENILE DELINQUENT
Today, as a result of peer group pressure, many a young teenager has been easily influenced down the road to juvenile delinquency. Peer group pressure is not the only reason why juvenile crime is rapidly rising, but many will agree that it is a factor.

Materials needed:
1. A cloth doll representing the child/teenager
2. Cooling Anger Incense
3. 4 red candles dressed with Courage and Success Oils
4. 2 white candles dressed with Power Oil
5. 1 pink candle dressed with Love Oil
6. 1 lt. blue candle dressed with Attraction Oil

(See Altar Diagram on following page).

1. Perform steps one through five as given in the Preliminary to Ritual. Your Psychic/Spiritual Development Herb Candle should be placed above the Holy Water.
2. Light White Candles #1 and 2, giving the following affirmation:
>   *These candles I light do symbolize,*
>   *the spiritual state, ____(name)____'s*
>   *source of life. May it grow in strength*

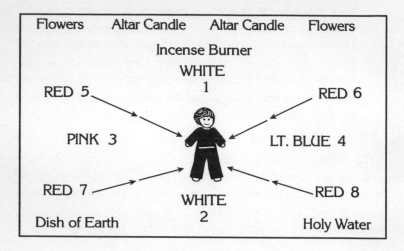

| Flowers | Altar Candle | Altar Candle | Flowers |

Incense Burner

WHITE 1

RED 5

RED 6

PINK 3

LT. BLUE 4

RED 7

WHITE 2

RED 8

Dish of Earth

Holy Water

with each new day. Always to keep
____(name)____ from going astray.

3. Light Pink Candle #3 as you affirm:
> Here is love which is in his/her
> life. Love is known, for love is
> shown to him/her by those who
> hold him/her dear.

4. Light Lt. Blue Candle #4 while affirming:
> Understanding comes his/her way,
> beginning now this very day.
> For he/she is wise and now can see,
> when others use him/her manipulatively.
> For this child will no longer be fooled,
> duped, tricked or led astray.

5. Light Red Candle #5, 6, 7, and 8 as you affirm:
> The parents have done all they could,
> to teach the child what's bad and good.
> But here is some strength which he/she
> will need,
> to follow his/her conscience in daily deeds.

A leader to be, not a follower see,
in doing what's right for humanity.

6. Allow the candles to burn a few minutes picturing the child being of positive help and assistance to others, or saying no and turning his/her back to that which is wrong as you affirm:

Strength and courage have come to
your side,
to resist the influence of those you see,
who would tempt you negatively.
For good do you live,
for good do you strive,
for your good name you do take pride.
Only that which is right,
remains forever within your sight.
A leader you'll be,
not a follower see,
in doing what's right
for humanity.

7. Allow the candles to burn a few more minutes and extinguish in reverse order of lighting them. Repeat daily moving the indicated candles an inch or so toward the doll until Red Candles #5, 6, 7, and 8 come within three inches of the doll. Wrap the doll in white linen and give to the child's parents for safekeeping.

OVERCOMING ADDICTIONS

Tobacco, drugs, alcohol, overeating—these are bad habits many would like to overcome within their life.
You will need the following materials:

1. a cloth doll representing the person who is a slave to a particular addiction
2. four white candles
3. two red candles

4. two black candles
5. some graveyard dust*
6. Rising Fame Incense
7. a bottle of Courage Oil
8. a bottle of Health Attracting Oil

In this ritual the black candles will represent the bad habit or addiction one would wish to rid themselves of; NOT to bring harm to another in any way. These two candles are not dressed, but sprinkled with the graveyard dirt.

The altar layout will be as follows:

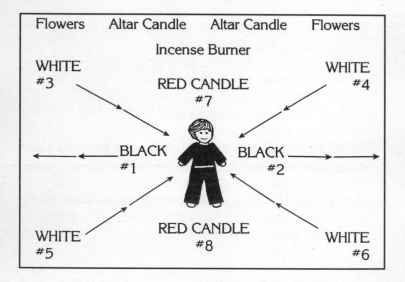

Flowers   Altar Candle   Altar Candle   Flowers

Incense Burner

WHITE #3

RED CANDLE #7

WHITE #4

BLACK #1   BLACK #2

WHITE #5

RED CANDLE #8

WHITE #6

1. Complete steps one through five as given in the Preliminary to Ritual. Your Psychic/Spiritual Development Herb Candle is placed above the Holy Water.
2. Light black candles #1 and 2 as you affirm:

---

*In Louisiana, graveyard dust is dust that has settled inside open tombs which is gathered simply by sweeping the inside of the tomb with a whisk broom.

> *Here is represented an addiction of*
> *____(name addiction)____ , this bad*
> *habit is what ____(name person)____*
> *strongly desires to overcome in*
> *his/her life. Already this bad*
> *habit grows weaker each day.*
> *Nevermore in his/her life to stay.*

3. LIGHT WHITE CANDLES #3, 4, 5, and 6 dressed with Courage Oil, again affirming:

> *Spiritual strength comes to your side,*
> *a strong faith within you resides. A*
> *conqueror you will be, over this enemy*
> *you see victory.*

4. Light red candles #7 and 8 dressed with Health Attracting Oil while affirming:

> *Further strength is at your side,*
> *as the victor, you'll stand high.*
> *Good health is a sign you'll see,*
> *that you have the victory.*

5. Allow the candles to burn a few moments, then chant the following:

> *Assured victory is yours,*
> *and conquered the enemy you've done*
> *your chore.*
> *For you are now truly free,*
> *from the bad habit that used to be.*

6. See in your mind the person completely free from his/her addiction, then blow out the two black candles. Repeat your chant, then extinguish the rest of the candles. Repeat, your chant, then extinguish the rest of the candles in reverse order of lighting them. Repeat this ritual every three days (moving the indicated candles) until satisfied. NOTE: Since you are working to remove a bad habit from your life or of another's it is best to begin this type or ritual during the waning phase of the moon.

TO WIN THE LOVE OF ANOTHER

Materials needed in this ritual:

1. 1 clay doll to represent the petitioner (the person requesting the ritual).
2. 1 clay doll to represent the person whose love is desired.
3. 2 red candles
4. 2 yellow candles
5. 1 orange candle
6. 1 pair of lodestones
7. 1 bottle of Attraction Oil
8. 1 bottle of Love Oil
9. 1 bottle of Courage Oil
10. Enticing Love Incense

NOTE: On one red candle write, "____(petitioner's name)____'s growing love for ____(other name)____". After this is written on the candle, then dress it with your Love Oil. This candle is to be tied to the back of the petitioner's doll with red thread. On the other red candle write, "____(other name)____'s growing love for ____(petitioner's name)____". Dress this candle with Love Oil and tie it to the back of the doll.

The two yellow candles are dressed with Attraction Oil. The orange candle is dressed with Courage Oil. Altar layout will be as diagram on following page.

1. Perform steps one through five as given in the Preliminary to Ritual. The Psychic and Spiritual Development Herb Candle should be placed above the Holy Water.
2. Light red candle #1 with the affirmation:
   Within ____(petitioner's name)____ a
   love does grow,
   a love that is strong,
   a love that will show.

```
Flowers     Altar Candle     Altar Candle     Flowers
                   Incense Burner
YELLOW CANDLE 1

Lodestone

RED CANDLE 1 &        RED CANDLE 2   ORANGE
Petitioner's Doll ←——— ←———— & Other Doll   CANDLE

Lodestone

YELLOW CANDLE 2
                          BOOK         Holy Water
```

3. Light red candle #2, giving the affirmation:

> In ____(other name)____'s heart the
> seeds of love are sown.
> As his/her love daily grows,
> ____(petitioner's name)____ , he/she
> calls his/her own.
> A love that is strong,
> A love that is bold.
> And in his/her arms,
> His/her love, he/she longs
> to hold.

4. Light the yellow candle 1 & 2 while affirming:

> Attraction on the right,
> attraction on the left,
> helps bring to ____(petitioner's name)____,
> The one he/she loves best.
> As the flame, attracts the moth,
> does this pair come together
> in a love which is not lost.

5. Light the orange candle giving the affirmation:

> *Encouragement comes to*
> *____(other name)____'s side,*
> *To seek out the love he/she*
> *can no longer hide.*

6. At this point you will send your own energy to give added strength to your ritual. Hold both hands up with palms facing toward the altar. With creative imagination, see the couple coming together, embracing one another, being in love. As you hold this mental picture in your mind, will your energy to flow as you chant:

> *Love growing between these two,*
> *their hearts beating love that's true.*
> *Thoughts attuned to one another,*
> *apart, they can live no longer.*
> *And as one,*
> *these two become.*
> *Flames of passion,*
> *and of yearning,*
> *in their hearts,*
> *steady burning.*
> *And as one,*
> *these two become.*

Repeat the chant, three, five, seven or nine times.

7. Allow the candles to burn for one hour. Extinguish the candles to burn for one hour. Extinguish the candles in reverse order to lighting them. Repeat daily, moving, red candle #2 and doll, one or two inches toward red candle #1 and petitioner's doll until both dolls touch. On the last day of this ritual the touching dolls are bound together with red ribbon. Wrap the dolls in clean white linen and give them to the petitioner to keep in a safe place.

8. The petitioner (if other than yourself) should burn a special herb candle for love daily. This individual should affirm while lighting the candle the following: "May the one I love see the true love I hold within and come to my

side". Or, if the petitioner is a man, he should read Chapter 6 in the Song of Solomon. A woman, should read Chapter 8 in the Song of Solomon. The daily ritual bath will consist of the following: a tablespoon of Blessed Salt into the bath water to which nine drops of Seduction Oil and seven drops of Love Oil has been added. Also, try to impress upon the man or woman that they should concentrate or think very hard on the one they love while they are taking the ritual bath. After taking the ritual bath, the individual should sprinkle Love Drawing Powder on their neck and chest. Extinguish the candle.

TO DEVELOP UNDERSTANDING

For this ritual you will need the following materials:

1. a clay doll to represent the petitioner
2. 1 yellow candle*
3. 2 light blue candles
4. 1 bottle of Attraction Oil
5. 1 bottle of Success Oil
6. Aura of Enchantment Incense

Since a yellow candle is used in this ritual we see that the petitioner wishes to develop understanding in his or her studies. On this candle write the nature of the studies, be it math, science, language etc. This candle should be tied to the back of the petitioner's doll.

On the candle representing the area that understanding is needed (in this case the yellow candle), anoint with Attraction Oil, the two light blue candles anoint with Success Oil.

Since a yellow candle is used in this ritual, we see that the petitioner wishes to develop understanding in his or her studies. On this candle write the nature of the studies, be it

---

*A different color candle will be used to represent the area in which we wish to develop understanding: yellow—studies, pink—friendships, purple—business,politics and white—politics and government, spiritual matters, light blue—medicine, red—life in general, red or pink—matters of love, orange—changes in life.

math, science, language etc. This candle should be tied to the back of the petitioner's doll.

On the candle representing the area that understanding is needed in (this case the yellow candle), anoint with Attraction Oil, the two light blue candles anoint with Success Oil.

Altar layout is as follows:

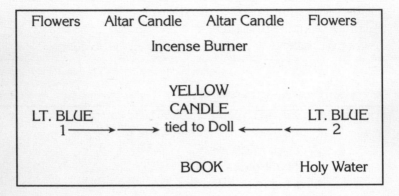

Flowers	Altar Candle	Altar Candle	Flowers
	Incense Burner		
	YELLOW CANDLE		
LT. BLUE 1 ——→—— →	tied to Doll ←——←		LT. BLUE 2
	BOOK	Holy Water	

1. Perform steps one through five as given in the Preliminary to Ritual. The psychic and Spiritual Development Herb Candle should be placed above the Holy Water.
2. Light the yellow candle giving the following affirmation:
   *Here is an area in life which
   understanding is greatly needed.
   Soon, will ____(petitioner's name)____
   ____learn to understand all there
   is related to ____(name the situation
   in which understanding is needed ____.*
3. Light the light blue candles 1 and 2 in order, while giving the following affirmation:
   *Light of knowledge, shine this way,
   dispelling ignorance today. As we
   learn, we understand,*

the truth revealed, with each
new day. Once was blind, but now
does see, as understanding
comes to thee.

Pause for a few moments and meditate on the petitioner. Think of the petitioner doing all that he or she can do to encourage greater understanding. Then repeat the affirmation:

Light of knowledge,
shine this way,
dispelling ignorance today.
As we learn, we understand,
the truth revealed,
with each new day.
Once was blind,
but now does see,
as understanding comes to thee.

Pause for a few moments, once again meditating on the petitioner. Then repeat the affirmation:

Light of knowledge,
shine this way,
dispelling ignorance today.
As we learn, we understand,
the truth revealed,
with each new day.
Once was blind,
but now does see,
as understanding comes to thee.

4. Allow the candles to burn for one hour. Extinguish them in reverse order of lighting them. Repeat daily, moving light blue candles # 1 and 2, one or two inches toward the yellow candle and petitioner's doll, until the candles touch the petitioner's doll.

5. The petitioner (if other than yourself) should burn a special Understanding Herb Candle, giving the following affir-

mation; "May this flame symbolize my growing understanding in ____(what you wish to understand)____", or read Psalm 133 from the Bible. In the daily bath water place a tablespoon of Blessed Salt and add nine drops of Attraction Oil. Burn Aura of Enchantment incense daily for seven days.

TO OBTAIN YOUR DESIRES

In this ritual you will need the following materials:
1. A clay doll to represent the petitioner
2. 3 candles representing the desire
3. 2 purple candles
4. 4 pink candles
5. 1 bottle of Success Oil
6. 1 bottle of Power Oil
7. Incense (see below for type)

NOTE: One candle representing the desire will be tied to the back of the doll representing the petitioner. Refer to the altar diagram for the placement of the other two candles and their use in the ritual. The color of this candle will change according to the desire:

MONEY ....3 green candles blessed and dressed with Money Drawing Oil, and burn Shower of Gold Incense.

HAPPINESS ....3 pink candles dressed with Happiness Oil, and burn Aura of Enchantment Incense.

GOOD LUCK ....3 green candles blessed and dressed with Lucky Life Oil, burn Leprechaun's Gold Incense.

SUCCESS ....3 orange candles blessed and dressed with Success Oil, and burn Rising Fame Incense.

HEALTH...............3 red candles blessed and dressed with Health Attracting Oil, and burn Glow of Health incense.

PROSPERITY ......3 green candles blessed and dressed with Success Oil, and burn Rising Fame Incense.

FORTUNATE.......3 orange candles blessed and dressed
DREAMS with Dream Oil, and burn Dreams of Prophesy Incense.

SPIRITUAL ....3 white candles blessed and dressed with
STRENGTH Power Oil, and burn Aura of Enchantment Incense.

In the altar layout candles 2, 3, 4 and 5 are blessed and dressed with Success Oil. Candles 6 and 7 are blessed and dressed with Power Oil.

Your altar layout will be as follows:

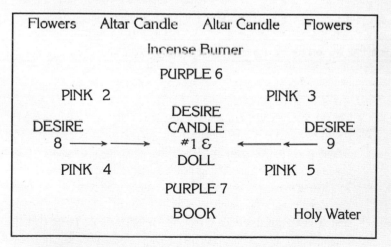

1. Perform steps one through five as given in the Preliminary to Ritual. The Psychic and Spiritual Development Herb Candle should be placed above the Holy Water.

2. Light the desire candle #1, giving the affirmation:

   Daily desire in ____(petitioner's
   name)____ grows,
   to have ____(name desire)____
   in his/her life to show.
   Soon, this reality he/she will know.

3. Light pink candles #2, 3, 4 and 5, giving the affirmation:

   Honor, love, surrounding you,
   as you daily live your life for
   the good.
   As this blessing soon comes to you,
   this fulfilled desire is a likelihood.

4. Light purple candles #6 and 7, while giving the affirmation:

   What you are seeking is seeking you.
   Here is the power to see it through.
   So the desire for ____(name desire)____
   can come to you.

5. Light desire candles #8 and 9, giving the affirmation:

   ____(name desire)____, coming to
   the fore,
   its strength increasing evermore.
   Fulfilled desire is in store,
   which you will have forevermore.

6. Mentally picture the petitioner doing all he/she can to bring the desire into his/her life, and finally having the desire in his/her life. If it is money, see the petitioner having the amount of money that is needed. If it is health, see the petitioner in a healthy state of being, etc. While holding this mental picture of the petitioner in your mind, place both hands up, palms facing the altar, and will your energy to flow forward as you chant:

   Energy flowing freely,
   giving added strength you see.
   Success growing steadily,

_____(name desire)_____ *is realized quickly.*
_____(name desire)_____ *coming to the
fore,*
_____(name desire)_____ *to have forevermore.*

7. Allow the candles to burn for 30 minutes. Extinguish
   them in reverse order of lighting them. Repeat daily for
   14 days.

Part II: Always try to get the person to work along with you in
the rituals.

MONEY ....Burn a special Money Herb Candle dressed
with Money Drawing Oil. As the candle is lit,
the following affirmation is given: "My needs
are fulfilled as I place my faith in God", or read
Psalm 41. In the bath place one tablespoon of
Blessed salt and nine drops of Money Drawing Oil. Daily sprinkle Money Drawing Powder on your neck and chest.

LOVE ....Burn daily a special Love Herb Candle dressed
with Love Attracting Oil. As the candle is lit,
give the following affirmation "May the one i
love see the true love I hold within and come
to my side", or a man should read Chapter 6
in the Song of Solomon and a woman should
read Chapter 8 in the Song of Solomon. In
the bath add a tablespoon of Blessed Salt
and nine drops of Seduction Oil. On your
neck and chest sprinkle Love Drawing Powder.

GOOD LUCK....Burn a special Luck Herb Candle blessed and
dressed with Lucky Life Oil. In the bath, place
four drops of Lucky Life Oil and five drops of
Power Oil. On the neck and chest apply Uncrossing Powder. As the candle is lit, the follow-

ing affirmation should be given: "May the light of good fortune shine upon me that I may see a more promising future", or read Psalm 62, verse 11, nine times.

SUCCESS ....Burn a special Success Herb Candle blessed and dressed with Success Oil. As the candle is lit, give the following affirmation: "As I live an orderly life, filled in God's righteousness, I will know success in my life", or read Psalm 95. In the bath add a tablespoon of blessed salt and nine drops of Success Oil. Sprinkle Uncrossing Powder on the neck and chest.

HEALTH ....Burn a special Herb Healing Candle blessed and dressed with Health Attracting Oil. Repeat the following affirmation as the candle is lit: "Let this flame flow forth the divine healing rays to restore my mind, body and soul to a state of perfect health", or read Psalm 38 on one day and Psalm 23 the next day, alternating days. In the bath place a tablespoon of blessed salt and nine drops of Health Attracting Oil.

PROSPERITY ......Burn a special Success Herb Candle blessed and dressed with Success Oil. Give the following affirmation: "Light the path which will lead me to a prosperous life", or read Psalm 41. In the bath add a tablespoon of blessed salt and nine drops of Success Oil. Sprinkle Uncrossing Powder on the neck and chest. Carry in your pocket a High John the Conqueror root.

SPIRITUAL ....Burn a special Spiritual and Psychic Power
STRENGTH   Herb Candle blessed and dressed with Blessing Oil. Give the following affirmation as

SPIRITUAL ....you light the candle; "May this light sym-
STRENGTH bolize the eternal love I hold for God. As I
Cont'd. live according to His teachings, I will surely
attain a higher spiritual level", or read Psalm
23. In the bath place a tablespoon of blessed
salt and add nine drops of Power Oil.

NOTE: This ritual should be performed daily, moving the desire candles #8 and 9 an inch or two in the direction of the arrows until they touch desire candle #1 and doll.

TO UNCROSS ANOTHER

In this ritual you will need the following materials:
1. a clay doll to represent the petitioner
2. 4 white candles
3. 1 black candle
4. graveyard dust
5. 1 bottle of Uncrossing Oil
6. Uncrossing Incense
7. 4 pieces of white paper with the individual's name written on them

The four white candles are blessed and dressed with Uncrossing Oil. Since the black candle will represent the crossed condition in this ritual it is neither blessed nor dressed. The graveyard dust will be used to sprinkle on this candle. The four pieces of paper will be placed under each of the white candles.

(See altar diagram on following page.)

1. Perform steps one through five as given in the Preliminary to Ritual. The Psychic and Spiritual Development Herb Candle should be placed above the Holy Water.

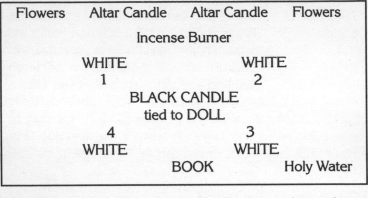

Flowers	Altar Candle	Altar Candle	Flowers

Incense Burner

WHITE 1   WHITE 2

BLACK CANDLE
tied to DOLL

4   3

WHITE   WHITE

BOOK   Holy Water

2. Anoint Uncrossing Oil on the forehead, throat, heart, above the naval and genitals of the doll as you chant:

Protection comes to you this day,
this crossed condition no longer
*   has sway.*
Returning this negativity,
to the one who has crossed thee.

If you have not previously tied the black candle to the back of the doll, then do so and place the doll and black candle in the center of the four white candles.

3. Light the black candle as you give the affirmation:

Surrounding ____(name of
*   petitioner)____*
is a crossed condition,
from which he/she desires to be set free.
Soon is dispelled,
This attacking energy.

4. Light the four white candles as you give the affirmation:

This fire and oil will do their best
to uncross and free you night and day.
From the north, east, south and west,
dispelling the evil sent your way.
Uncrossed and happy, you will be,

set free from attacking energy.

5. Blow out the black candle. Allow the four white candles to burn for one hour. During this time think of the petitioner as being set free from the crossed condition. Picture in your mind the petitioner surrounded with a white light. Extinguish the four white candles in reverse order of lighting them. Repeat the ritual daily for seven days.

6. Somewhere in the victim's house or yard there will be a gris-gris bag for evil or a small conjure ball. The conjure ball is basically the same as a gris-gris bag, except it is made from black wax and is covered with black feathers. Whenever the victim comes in close contact with the gris-gris bag or conjure ball, his or her aura will pick up the negative vibrations which the gris-gris bag or conjure ball is linking to him or her through a crossing ritual. Therefore it is essential that this gris-gris bag or conjure ball be found, to assure that the crossed condition does not begin all over again. When the gris-gris bag or conjure ball is found it is placed in a small wooden coffin.

7. In a secret spot in the woods, dig a small grave. Completely sprinkle the grave with your Holy Water. Place the small coffin with its evil contents in this grave. Pour a small amount of gasoline over this grave and set it on fire. While the coffin is burning, chant:

> *Consumed by this mighty flame,*
> *your evil shall no longer reign.*
> *As all things come to an end,*
> *your victim now does smile again.*
> *As ____(name of individual)____*
> *begins his/her life anew,*
> *your harm to him/her,*
> *you no longer can do.*
> *I send you to a place of rest,*
> *leaving your victim*

to a life that is best.
At the end of each line sprinkle some spirits of ammonia
into the fire. When the fire has died out, cover the grave.
Do not look back as you walk away from it.
8. At the end of the seven days, the doll is wrapped in clean
   white linen and given to the petitioner to keep in a safe
   place.

The petitioner should do the following:
1. Burn daily for one hour a special Herb Uncrossing Candle, which has been blessed and dressed with Uncrossing Oil.
2. In the bath water place a tablespoon of blessed salt and
   add nine drops of Uncrossing Oil.
3. To the scrub water add Louisiana Essence of Van Van
   wash and scrub down the floors and front steps of the
   house.

Mix the following solution to give to the petitioner:
1. 4 oz. of water
2. 4 oz. of vinegar
3. 2 tbsp. blessed salt
4. 1 tbsp. jalop powder (powdered John the
   Conqueror root)
5. 1 tbsp. powdered basil leaves
6. 1 tbsp. powdered five-finger grass

Divide this mixture in two. Half of the mixture is to be
sprinkled in every corner of the house. The other half of
the mixture is divided again in half; one half is placed at
the front door and the other half is placed at the back
door. Tack a bay leaf in every corner of the house as it is
sprinkled with the solution. This will help make any
future attacks more difficult. Plus it will help remove any
negative vibrations which could attach themselves to the
home.

CONCERNING THE HOME

If you are moving into a new home (or even an old apartment building) it is always wise to cleanse the area of any negative vibrations left by previous tenets or negative thoughts built up by dissatisfied workers on a new building. The aura of all buildings has always been molded by the thoughts and emotions of those who spend a lot of time within their walls.

With the busy pace of our everyday life, every working man and woman relishes the blessing of having a calm and loving home to return to at the end of each day. You too can have a tranquil and loving atmosphere in your home if you cleanse the home's aura of all negative vibrations. This process is what we call "Dressing a Home". It can also be used for removing negative vibrations within a business.

1. Open all windows and doors to the home or building.
2. Thoroughly scrub down the floors with the following solution:
   > 1 oz. Louisiana Van Van Oil
   > ¼ cup ammonia
   > 1 tbsp. Blessed Sea Salt
   > to one bucket of water
3. After the floors are scrubbed mix the following solution:
   > 4 oz. water
   > 4 oz. cider vinegar
   > 1 tbsp. Blessed Sea Salt
   > 1 tbsp. jalop powder (powdered John the Conqueror root)
   > 1 tbsp. powdered basil leaves
   > 1 tbsp. powdered rosemary leaves

Divide this mixture in two parts. Take half of the mixture and sprinkle every corner of the home. As you sprinkle, you should be chanting or praying for the negative psychic energy to be removed from the premises. The other part of this mixture is again divided in two and placed in jars, cup, etc. One jar is to be put at the front door and the other jar is put at the back door.

4. Having done this, you must cense the house or building, using Le Diable S'en Va Incense. Cense each corner of the house while chanting or praying for the negative vibes to be removed.

Now that you have cleansed the aura of your home, you may wish to do something to keep frustrations, quarrels and conflict, which could cause dissension among the members of the household, to a minimum. Follow these instructions:

Using your basic altar layout, bring to your altar the following:

1. Cooling Anger Incense
2. 3 pink candles, dressed with Love Oil
3. A piece of white paper on which is written a member of the household's name (e.g. if there are four members in the home, you will have four pieces of paper with one name written on each).

The only change you will make from your basic altar layout will be the placements of your incense burner. Place it in the center of your altar. The three pink candles dressed with Love Oil are placed around the incense burner in the form of a triangle with one point upright.

PINK CANDLE
1

CENSOR

PINK CANDLE   PINK CANDLE
2   3

1. Follow steps one through five as given in the Preliminary

to Ritual. Your Psychic/Spiritual Development Herb Candle is put above your Holy Water.

2. Light your pink candles #1, 2 and 3 in their proper order. As you light your candles chant:

> *Fires of love burning bright,*
> *instill within these hearts tonight,*
> *love that's true, love that's right.*
> *To be ready of help and concern might,*
> *always to act in ways that are right.*

Continue your chanting three, five, seven or nine times.

3. At this point, take a slip of paper on which you have written a family member's name, and place it in the incense burner to burn as you chant:

> *Peace and love are known to thee,*
> *within the home you bring harmony.*
> *No thoughts of anger do you show,*
> *toward the ones who love you so.*
> *Peace and love are known to thee,*
> *as you strive for harmony.*

When the paper is completely burned put a quarter teaspoon of Cooling Anger Incense in your censor. Go on with the next piece of paper and burn it in the incense burner while using the chant until all pieces of paper are burned. You will find that doing this ritual at least once a month will greatly improve the harmony and cooperation of the family unit. Remember, a house divided does not stand.

AGAINST DOMESTIC VIOLENCE

Materials needed:

1. a small jar with a screw top (the small spice jars bought in the grocery are ideal) which will symbolize the home
2. a piece of rede cloth cut in the shape of a heart

3. some brand-new sewing needles (one for each member of the family)
4. a few strands of hair from each member of the family
5. a two ounce mixture of equal parts honey and sweet wine
6. ¼ tsp. of the following herbs: vervain, passion flower, dulse, and a piece of John the Conqueror root
7. Cooling Anger Incense
8. two pink candles
9. two light blue candles
10. one red candle

NOTE: Since the needles will symbolize each member of the family, the strand of hair belonging to that person is to be passed through the eye of the needle that will represent that individual. Each needle is to be named and consecrated as given in step four of the doll consecration ritual (page 56). A last word: be sure to tie the strand of hair which you have passed through the needle's eye to prevent it from detaching itself from the needle.

Please arrange layout of your altar as in diagram on following page:

1. Perform steps one through five as given in the Preliminary to Ritual. Your Psychic/Spiritual Development Herb Candle should be placed above the Holy Water.
2. Take each of the needles and fasten them to the heart cut from red cloth. Place this in your jar.
3. Put your herbs into the jar, then pour your mixture of honey and sweet wine over the herbs until the jar is filled. If you like, you may chant the following while doing steps two and three:

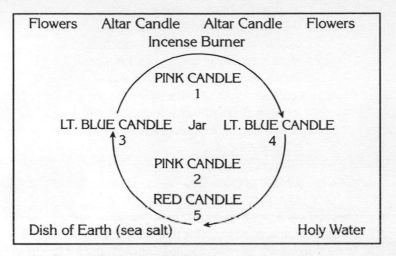

In peace and love,
the family will be,
living together in harmony.
In peace and love as it should be,
each member strives for harmony.
As the home is a paradise of love,
each working together harmoniously.

4. Light pink candles #1 and 2 as you affirm:
Love, shine your light from above,
make this home a paradise of love.
All for one and one for all,
the motto for this home of love.
These hearts filled with love we see,
care for each other constantly.
Always ready to do what's right,
never to harm or the other fight.
Love, shine your light from above,
to make this house a paradise of love.

5. Light lt. blue candles #3 and 4 while affirming:
Peace and love are known to thee,

as you daily strive for harmony.
All working together constantly,
within the home, living peacefully.
Peace and love are known to thee,
as all daily strive for harmony.

6. Light red candle #5, giving the affirmation:
Here is strength which comes
to the home, to strengthen the bonds
of love that is
shown.
To live peacefully,
all work earnestly,
making this house a home, you see.

Allow the candles to burn for a few minutes. This ritual is to be done daily, moving the red candle three inches in a clockwise circle around the filled jar, two pink candles and two lt. blue candles, until the red candle returns to its original position below pink candle two.

7. At the completion of the ritual, cap the jar and keep it in a safe place in the home or on your own altar or place of daily prayer.

THE SUCCESSFUL BUSINESS

Thinking of starting your own business? Is your present business moving at a slow rate due to the economic situation or too much competition? Certainly we want to protect our investment of time and money. This can be done if the following instructions are carried out.

First of all, you will need to purify/cleanse your place of business of all negative vibrations from the past by following the procedure outlined for "Cleansing Your Home".

Gather your materials on a Thursday (this day is preferable because it is ruled by Jupiter and governs success in your chosen career) during the waxing phase of the moon.

1. a yellow candle dressed with Attraction Oil
2. a green candle dressed with Success Oil
3. a purple candle dressed with Success Oil
4. a batch of business drawing wash (Note: if for some reason you cannot get squill root, then substitute ¼ oz. each of the following; chamomile, basil, parsley, and peony).
5. a pair of lodestones
6. John the Conqueror root
7. some coin and paper money
8. a piece of button snake root
9. some mint

Place items 5, 6, 7, 8, and 9 in a small bowl. In a corner of your place of business, set up a small table, preferably in an area where people will not come near it. On this table you will place your candles and filled bowl according to the following diagram:

YELLOW
CANDLE

PURPLE CANDLE   GREEN CANDLE

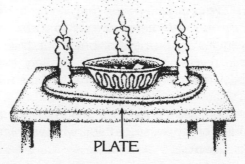

PLATE

1. Light yellow candle while chanting:

> *The aura of attraction building strong,*
> *people coming all day long.*
> *To this place their needs fulfilled,*
> *in harmony with our wills.*
> *Here the attraction is built strong,*
> *people now come all day long.*

2. Light the green candle as you chant:
> *Growing, growing, steadily,*
> *this business prospers, all can see.*
> *growing, growing, steadily,*
> *this business has prosperity.*

3. *Light the purple candle while chanting:*
> *Of all the places that there be,*
> *this one makes progress with glee.*
> *Working each day joyfully,*
> *for progress we clearly see.*

4. Allow the candles to burn as you begin to use your business drawing wash. When using and making your wash you should chant:
> *Many customers we have,*
> *and then some to spare.*
> *Here people know they're treated well,*
> *with respect and great care.*
> *And quickly now, they come here,*
> *our customers we love so dear.*

5. The candles are burned for one hour, then extinguish them in reverse order of their lighting. Repeat every Thursday during the waxing phase of the moon.

Suggestion: It is a good idea to add to your bowl some toy figures of people, since this is what you want to attract to your business.

Chapter Four

THE EVIL EYE

The evil eye, also known as the glance of malice, has been known to all people. The ancient Celts believed that those possessed with the evil eye could blight whole crops at a glance, or make cows dry up and no longer give milk. When a person or domestic farm animal became sick, the glance of malice was suspect of being put upon them.

The evil eye is just as common today as it was centuries ago. In fact, there are many people who use it and are not aware of doing so. The Gospel of Mark 7:22-23, in the King James Version of the Bible, mentions the evil eye as one of the things projected from the hearts of men which defiles man, probably because its roots are envy, jealousy, and possessiveness which are negative emotions.

There is an old belief that the eyes send out rays of energy. The strength of this energy will vary among different people. Therefore, the glance of malice is transmitted to another when the energy shooting out from the eyes is negatively charged by one of the three emotions mentioned while looking at the individual. No one is really free from the curse of the evil eye, because this negative energy affects people, animals, and objects. We are constantly coming in contact with people who may be envious of our good fortune in life. A co-worker may be jealous because we are climbing the ladder of success within the company instead of staying at his or her level.

Our normal senses of touch, taste, smell, and hearing are not programmed to alert us when we are being sent the evil eye in its early stages. It is only after repeated attacks that the conscious mind begins to alert us that there may be something wrong. The most common symptoms associated with the glance of malice takes the form of minor illness, again making it hard to detect, because you don't suspect the evil eye as the cause. Only those who have trained themselves in auric sight can actually see its effects upon the aura before the minor physical illnesses occur. Regardless of these physical symptoms associated with the evil eye, left untreated over a period of time, the victim becomes accident prone and injures him/herself.

Treatment for the evil eye is in two parts and is quite simple, yet effective: a) taking a spiritual/aura cleansing bath to remove what negative energy the aura has picked up already and b) wearing the crossbones amulet for protection from future attacks.

The Bath

Fill the bathtub half full with warm water. To this water add one tablespoon each of Blessed Sea Salt and clear household ammonia. As you enter the tub, bring with you a small bowl, cup or glass to pour the water over you. As you are pouring the water over yourself, imagine all negative energy being washed off your aura. Once this is done, imagine yourself being completely filled up from head to toe with white light. let this white light extend from your body to a radius of about three feet, also extending above your head and below your feet. While you are in this bath, completely immerse yourself in the water about every three minutes. This spiritual/aura cleansing bath should last nine minutes with a total of three immersions. When you get out of the bathtub you may towel dry your hair but let the bath water air dry on your skin. This way the cleansing effect will stay with you for a period of twenty-four hours.

The Crossbones Amulet

The crossbones, as we will call it, is made at your altar. The amulet itself is made from two small bones taken from chicken wings. The chicken bones actually absorb and hold negativity. The bones are tied together with black thread in the shape of a solar cross (an equal armed cross). The procedure is as follows:

Using your basic altar layout, bring with you the following: two bones, black thread, a white candle, a bottle of Power Oil, Gris-Gris Faible Incense.

1. Light your altar candles.
2. Light your incense.
3. Light your white candle dressed with Power Oil. Pray that the individual who will wear the crossbones will grow in spiritual strength and enlightenment.
4. Begin tying the two bones together with the black thread as you chant:

   The crossbones will work here,
   absorb and hold negativity.
   Into your marrow,
   it goes in thee;
   all evil and negativity.

5. Consecrate the amulet with this procedure. Sprinkle with Holy Water as you say:

   With water do I consecrate this
   amulet, an instrument which will
   absorb and hold negative energy
   sent to its wearer.

Sprinkle the amulet with salt as you affirm:

   With earth do I consecrate this

> amulet, an instrument which will
> absorb and hold negative energy
> sent to its wearer.

Pass the amulet through the candle flame as you affirm:

> With fire do I consecrate this
> amulet, an instrument which will
> absorb and hold negative energy
> sent to its wearer.

Pass the amulet through the incense while affirming:

> With air do I consecrate this
> amulet, an instrument which will
> absorb and hold negative energy
> sent to its wearer.

Now that your amulet is completed, it should be worn over your heart next to your skin. Daily wear this amulet until it begins to feel heavy upon your heart chakra. When this feeling of heaviness occurs, you must stop wearing the amulet. The crossbones have reached their maximum in absorbing negative energy, like a sponge that can soak up just so much water and that's it. Since the excess negative energy being sent to you will not be able to enter the bones, it will have no choice but to attach itself to your aura. Once the old amulet is removed, it must be discarded. The safest method of doing this is through ritual.

Discarding the Old Amulet

Using your basic altar layout, bring with you the following: your old amulet, the remainder of the white candle you used when you made the amulet, a sheet of white paper.

1. Light Altar Candles.
2. Light your incense (Aura of Enchantment is recommended).
3. Light your white candle.
4. Sprinkle white paper with Holy Water.
5. Place the old crossbones amulet on the paper and begin

to fold the amulet in the paper.

6. Take your white candle and let the wax drip on the paper until it is completely sealed with the white wax as you affirm:

> *Crossbones you've served me well,*
> *negative energy within you swells.*
> *Now it's time, I put you to rest,*
> *for you have now done your best.*

When the paper is completely covered with wax, the amulet can be discarded in the garbage. Follow with a bath.

Chapter Five

FOLK SPELLS AND MISCELLANEOUS

TO CONTROL ANOTHER

Take a High John the Conqueror Root and anoint it with John the Conqueror Oil. On a piece of brown paper, write the name of the person you wish to control/conquer and soak the paper in Controlling Oil. When the paper is dry, wrap it around the High John the Conqueror root and tie with purple thread.

TO BIND A LOVER TO YOU

Take a small mirror which your lover has looked into. Without looking into the mirror, break it into small pieces. Bury the broken mirror in your yard or in a flower pot you keep in your home. Every Friday, sprinkle the spot with a tea made from Spikenard Herb while repeating the name of your lover.

TO CAUSE YOUR ENEMY TO LEAVE

Take a small jar. Write your enemy's name nine times on a piece of paper and put this in the jar. Fill the jar with Four Thieves Vinegar and throw it into a river.

TO MAKE A MAN LOVE YOU

It's an established practice for some women to mix some of their menstrual blood in the food of the man they love.

TO OVERCOME AN ENEMY

Take a brown candle and write your enemy's name three times on it. Place it in a bowl filled with brown sugar. Light the candle and affirm; "Your hostility, I'll overcome. In days of nine, your friendship is mine." Do this before you go to bed. Allow the candle to burn itself out while you sleep. In the morning take what is left of the candle wax and the brown sugar and throw it in your enemy's yard. Do this for nine consecutive days without fail.

WORKING WITH MAGICK LAMPS

The type of lamp used to make these magick lamps is the hurricane or kerosene lamp. Like the gris-gris bags, the magick lamps are made for many purposes. The basic fuel used in making these lamps is a blend of castor oil, olive oil and kerosene. Here you will use two thirds kerosene to one third oil mixture. To this basic fuel mixture is added other ingredients which are analogous to the work being done. Here you will add diverse ingredients such as: magnets, essential oils, herbs, pepper, red wine, etc.

When properly made, the lamps have excellent results. The results obtained from working with lamps is best when prayers are said as you fill the lamp with more fuel each day at the same time. Once the lamp is lit, it cannot be extinguished until satisfaction is obtained. If you don't need to fill the hurricane lamp as you say your prayer, then the lamp is moved in a circular motion, clockwise, as you repeat your desire. The prayer which has always been given to use with the lamp has always been directed to a particular Saint (Catholic influence).

Here, I see no reason why a person of the pagan influence can't use their own prayer invoking the aid of a pagan God or Goddess.

THE HEALTH LAMP

This lamp, as with all other lamps, will contain a universal fluid mixture plus a magnet, a personal object from the person the lamp is for, or their name written on parchment paper cut in the form of a cross. You will place this at the bottom of your lamp and pour your fuel over this and the magnet. Since this lamp is being made for health, we will add the following; one Bottle of Health Attracting Oil and one half teaspoon of the following herbs: heal-all, peppermint, eucalyptus, etc. (a combination of five different healing herbs or four herbs and five-finger grass). The prayer used is directed to Our Lady of Lourdes (used by the French) or St. Joseph (used by the Italians).

To correctly use the lamp, the flame must not be extinguished once it is lit, and as you say your prayer and state your desire, you must shake the lamp in a clockwise direction to get the ingredients in the lamp moving in a clockwise direction to get the ingredients in the lamp moving in a clockwise direction. Again this must be done daily and at the same time each day until satisfied.

THE LOVE LAMP

To your basic fuel add the following: one bottle of Love Oil, five herbs associated with love or four herbs and some five-finger grass. Use a prayer to Saint Anne.

THE JUSTICE LAMP

Good for court cases and legal matters. Add the following: galangal root, yellow dock, snake root, carnation, and five-finger grass, one bottle of Friendly Judge Oil.

Say a prayer to St. Basil.

THE SUCCESS LAMP

To this lamp add the following; one bottle Success Oil and five herbs associated with success, or four herbs and five-finger grass. A prayer to St. Anthony is used here.

THE PROTECTION LAMP

Add one bottle of Protection Oil and five herbs of protective qualities or four herbs and five-finger grass. Pray to the Guardian Angel, St. Michael, or St. Barbara.

THE QUICK HELP LAMP

Add one bottle of Lucky Life Oil and five herbs associated with success or four herbs and five-finger grass. St. Expedite is who you would pray for assistance from.

THE PEACEFUL HOME LAMP

Add Baume du commandeur, one bottle of Peaceful Home Oil, passion flower, honey, mistletoe, jasmine flowers, orris root, and John the Conqueror root. Ask St. Raymond for his assistance. He is the one to pray to as you make your desire known.

THE SELF-IMPROVEMENT LAMP

Add one bottle of Blessing Oil and five herbs related to success. Pray to St. Mary Magdalene for assistance as you state your desire.

THE WORK LAMP

Used when one is looking for employment. To this lamp you will need to add something connected with the type of work you're seeking, e.g. for carpentry work add nails, for hospital work add basic medicines; it can even be a picture connected with the type of work you are seeking. One bottle of Attraction Oil and four herbs associated with success. Pray to St. Joseph as you make your request for employment.

NOTE: Some practitioners will add food coloring to the fuel to make it the color associated with the desire. Pink or red for love, purple for work, light blue for protection, red for health, orange for success, etc.

THE SWEET BOTTLE

On a popsicle stick, write your full name. On the other side of the popsicle stick, write another person's full name. Get a jar big enough to put the popsicle stick inside and fill the jar with water, honey and sugar. Seal up the lid of the jar tight so that its contents can't spill out. In your mind get a clear image of the person whose name you have written on the popsicle stick opposite your own. Shake the bottle as you chant three, five, seven or nine times:

> *Sweet, sweet,*
> *thoughts of me,*
> *you will think,*
> *constantly.*

It is said that each time you shake the bottle, the person will think sweet thoughts of you.

NEW YEAR'S PROSPERITY RITUAL

It is an established custom to eat cabbage, blackeye peas and rice in Southern Louisiana on New Year's Day. On New Year's Eve, after the supper dishes are washed and put away the kitchen table is set in the following manner: on the table is placed a dollar bill and a silver dollar. A green candle dressed with Money Drawing Oil is placed over the money. Around the money and candle, place the cabbage, black-eyed peas, rice, salt and any other seasonings to be used to cook the New Year's Day meal. A circle of salt is made around the food and candle. The candle is lit and allowed to burn itself out. While the candle is burning, prayers for prosperity for the New Year are said over this. All of this is left on the table overnight with the belief that the spirit of the New Year will bless the food as it passes.

On New Year's Day, as you are cutting the cabbage up for cooking, a small piece of cabbage leaf (usually the outer green leaf) is wrapped in wax paper and given to each member of the family to carry in their wallets, purse or even put under their mattress for the remainder of the year. The silver dollar is cooked in with the cabbage. After the cabbage is cooked, the silver dollar is saved to use again next year. Some families will put a dime in with the cabbage, believing that whoever finds the dime on their plate while eating will have extra good luck throughout the year.

The salt that was used to make a circle around the food and candle is thrown out the front door to chase away bad luck.

TO ELIMINATE A RIVAL
Purchase a beef tongue and make a split in it. On a piece of paper write nine times the name of your lover and the name of the person you suspect is your rival. Insert this paper in the split you made in the beef tongue. Sprinkle in with it a mixture of pepper, and ground chicory. Take nine new pins and close up the split made in the beef tongue. Place the tongue in the oven and roast it as you chant:

> ____(name of lover)____ ,
> you will no longer be
> with ____(name of rival)____

I say to thee.
Bitterness between you two,
spoils this love
you think is true.
When this beef tongue
is well done,
the end to your romance
has begun.

Repeat this chant three, five, seven or nine times as you picture in your mind the two going their separate ways. Once
your lover has eaten this tongue, the spell will begin to take
effect. Discord the leftover to rot away.

FORMULAS

**INCENSES
OILS
POWDERS
WASHES**

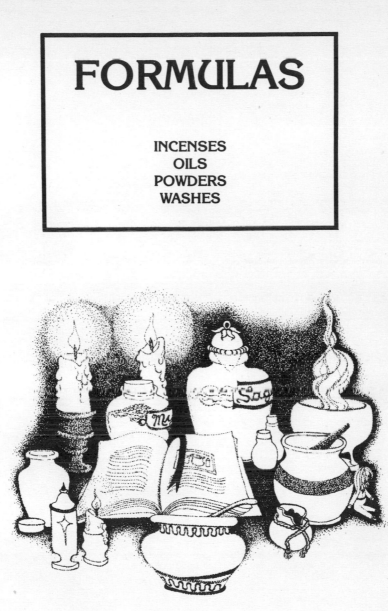

Chapter Six

INCENSE

Many ancient writings clearly indicate that the use of incense has been used in connection with religious and magickal practices throughout the world. The ancients believed that certain scents had the quality to attract good spirits and to dispel the evil ones. Incense was burned not only to purify a place dedicated to God, but also to neutralize the offensive odor from burnt offerings.

There is an old belief that prayers were carried upward to the Gods with the rising incense smoke. This same belief was held by many American Indian tribes in connection with their sacred peace pipe. In my opinion, the Indian peace pipe was a method of burning incense during ceremonies because they often mixed herbs with a little tobacco.

Aside from this, incense helps to create an atmosphere that is more conducive to proper meditation and devout prayer.

In the incense recipes which follow, you will be using some liquid ingredients by the dram, ¼ dram, etc. Therefore I'm including a handy conversion table.

⅛ fl. oz. = 1 dram = ½ tsp. plus ⅛ tsp.
¼ fl. oz. = 2 drams = ½ tbsp.
½ fl. oz. = 4 drams = 1 tbsp.

¾ fl. oz. = 6 drams = 1 tbsp. plus ½ tbsp.

1 fl. oz. = 8 drams = 2 tbsp.

The incense recipes I give are burned in the traditional method by placing the incense on a hot charcoal in your incense burner. In mixing them, powder all the solid ingredients and mix them well with your mortar and pestle. Mix all the liquid ingredients and dissolve the saltpeter in them. Slowly add the liquid ingredients to your powdered herbs. Spread in a tin pan or plastic container and allow to dry for thirty minutes to an hour. When dry, simply crumble up and you have your incense.

TINCTURE OF BENZOIN

In many of the recipes that follow, you will use tincture of benzoin. You can make your own as follows:

Power two ounces of benzoin gum and add 4 oz. of water and 12 oz. of alcohol. Keep this mixture tightly capped and bottled for two weeks and shake daily. If you prefer, a teaspoon of glycerin may be added. After two weeks strain and bottle the liquid for use.

ENTICING LOVE INCENSE

Try this incense in your rituals designed to attract and hold love. Can also be burned periodically to keep an aura of love about the home.

1 oz. rose petals

¼ oz. sweet bugle (calamus root)

½ oz. cinnamon

¼ oz. anise seed

¼ oz. frankincense

1 oz. powdered sandalwood

¼ tsp. saltpeter

2 drams tincture of benzoin

1 dram Seduction Oil

AURA OF ENCHANTMENT INCENSE

This is a formula which you can use for daily meditation and prayer.

¼ oz. bayberry herb
½ oz. powdered sandalwood
1 oz. frankincense
¼ oz. anise seed
¼ oz. powdered myrrh
¼ tsp. saltpeter
1 dram gardenia oil
2 drams tincture of benzoin

SHOWER OF GOLD

This incense is to be used in rituals pertaining to matters of money and prosperity.

1 oz. bayberry herb
1 oz. powdered sandalwood
1 oz. powdered frankincense
¼ oz. powdered myrrh
¼ tsp. saltpeter
1 dram cinnamon oil
2 drams tincture of benzoin

GLOW OF HEALTH

An incense formula used in rituals designed to attract or maintain good health.

½ oz. bayberry herb
1 oz. powdered sandalwood
1 oz. carnation petals
½ oz. rose petals
¼ tsp. saltpeter
2 drams tincture of benzoin

BON VOYAGE INCENSE

Use this formula in rituals to drive away those who are

troublesome to you. It can also be used in rituals to break up undesired relationships.

    1 oz. jalop powder
    ½ oz. rosemary herb
    ¼ oz. patchouli leaves
    1 tbsp. brimstone (sulphur)
    3 tbsps. ginger
    ¼ tsp. saltpeter
    2 drams tincture of benzoin

GRIS-GRIS FAIBLE INCENSE

This incense formula may be used in your rituals to destroy an enemy's power to harm you. Can also be used as an "Uncrossing Incense".

    1 oz. powdered sandalwood
    ½ oz. powdered bay leaves
    ½ oz. powdered dill seed
    1 tsp. asafoetida
    ¼ tsp. saltpeter
    1 dram Uncrossing Oil
    2 drams of tincture of benzoin

LE DIABLE S'EN VA INCENSE

Try this formula in your exorcism rituals. For removing negative thoughtforms within a building and heavy negative vibrations.

    ¼ tsp. powdered asafoetida
    1 oz. powdered frankincense
    ½ oz. powdered rosemary
    1 tbsp. powdered vanillin
    ¼ oz. jalop powder
    ¼ oz. basil leaves
    ¼ tsp. saltpeter
    2 drams tincture of benzoin
    1 dram Uncrossing Oil

RISING FAME INCENSE

A success incense. Use in rituals to attract wanted success and prosperity in your endeavors.

½ oz. powdered sandalwood
1 oz. cinnamon
½ oz. frankincense
¼ oz. powdered myrrh
¼ oz. powdered orris root
1 dram Attraction Oil
2 drams tincture of benzoin

PROPHETIC DREAMS

Use this formula as an incense to use in rituals for bringing about prophetic dreams. To burn while practicing divination or attempting astral projection.

½ oz. powdered sandalwood
¼ oz. bayberry herb
½ oz. rose petals
¼ oz. lavender
¼ oz. orris root (powdered)
1 oz. grated lemon peel
¼ tsp. saltpeter
1 dram frankincense oil
2 drams tincture of benzoin

COOLING ANGER INCENSE

An incense to use in rituals designed to calm down those who are angry and quarrelsome, heal unhappy marriages, etc. Can be burned periodically in the home to keep family members cooperating with one another.

1 oz. powdered passion flower
1 oz. powdered orris root
½ oz. powdered rose petals
½ oz. dark brown sugar

¼ tsp. saltpeter
1 dram of honey
2 drams tincture of benzoin

LEPRECHAUN'S GOLD INCENSE

To help attract good luck use the following mixture:
1 oz. cinnamon
1 oz. powdered sandalwood
¼ oz. powdered frankincense
¼ oz. bayberry herb
½ anise seed
½ oz. grated orange peel
¼ tsp. saltpeter
1 dram Louisiana Van Van oil
2 drams tincture of benzoin

UNCROSSING INCENSE

This is a basic uncrossing incense. Some practitioners recommend that this incense be burned near an open window for nine consecutive nights.
½ oz. powdered frankincense
1 oz. powdered dragon's blood
1 oz. powdered sandalwood
¼ tsp. saltpeter
1 dram of gardenia oil
2 drams tincture of benzoin

CIRCLE OF PROTECTION INCENSE

An incense formula to use in rituals designed to protect a person, home, or place of business from evil influences.
1 oz. powdered sandalwood
½ oz. powdered five-finger grass
¼ oz. powdered frankincense
¼ oz. grated orange peel
¼ tsp. saltpeter
1 dram of gardenia oil
2 drams tincture of benzoin

Chapter Seven

ANOINTING OILS

Floral and herbal scented oils still play an extremely important role in the world of magick. The ancients believed that certain odors had various effects on people and objects. From this thought, the practice of anointing with scented oils has been established in religious and magick ceremonies.

While applying the oil, it is important to concentrate upon the effect the oil is believed to have. After concentrating upon the desired effect, touch or hold the person or object with your right hand (left, if you are left-handed) and visualize the person or object completely surrounded by a white light.

To make your own anointing oil, start with a good vegetable oil base. Virgin Olive oil is fine, or you can use dipropylene glycol. Into your mortar and pestle pour two ounces of oil, and add two tablespoons of your herb or mixture and crush the herb or mixture into the oil. Store your bottle of oil in a previously consecrated dark place for three days. On the fourth day, check to see if the oil has absorbed the scent of the herb, mixture, or flower. If the oil has a weak scent, use a piece of cheesecloth and strain the oil. Add two more tablespoons of your herb, mixture, or flower to the oil. If necessary add a little more olive oil to bring the first oil back to two ounces. Store for three more days. Repeat this process until the scent of the oil is as strong as you like. With some of the herb mixtures as given in the following recipes, the first three days will produce a strong scented oil. Some flowers and herbs have a weak scent and it is necessary to repeat the process of scenting the oil.

Traditionally, you would chant over the oil a rhyme containing the purpose for which the oil is made each evening until the oil is complete. When you chant over your oil, hold the palms of both hands over it and direct your energy to flow into the oil. When you have finished making your oil, chant your rhyme over it a last time as you strain the herb, mixture, or flower from the oil.

With some of these anointing oil recipes it is necessary to put a piece of root, herb or lodestone in the bottle of oil as a finished product. In some, a root or herb is optional (i.e., if you want to, add a bit of root or herb to the oil) and this will be mentioned as optional in the recipe.

All of the anointing oils in this book are ideal to use in dressing candles. Some practitioners use them in other ways, and this will be mentioned as the recipe is given.

In some of the following formulas, gardenia flowers are used. Because of the sub-tropical climate of Louisiana, gardenias grow well. If for some reason gardenia is unobtainable or too expensive in your geographical area, you can substitute jasmine flowers.

In all of the following oil formulas, a few drops of tincture of benzoin can be added to prevent your oil from becoming rancid.

ATTRACTION OIL

Worn when looking for a mate. Anoint on your forehead, below the heart and above the naval. It is said that this oil will help to give you a more magnetic personality if a few drops are added to the bath water once a week. Said to help attract good luck when anointed in your shoes.

> *Mix equal parts of loveage herb and grated lemon peel or lemon flowers. Add two tablespoons of this mixture to two ounces of oil. A small piece of lodestone is added to each bottle of oil made.*

BANKRUPT OIL

Said to force an enemy to go broke. It is used in rituals designed to force someone to spend their money. This oil can be anointed on charms made to bring bad luck, and placed in a business to make the business go bankrupt.

> *Put two tablespoons of powdered devil's shoestring in two ounces of oil. OPTIONAL: add one small piece of devil's shoestring to each bottle of oil made.*

BLESSING OIL

Use this oil to purify or bless your altar, candlesticks, incense burner, etc.

> *Mix two parts of frankincense and one part of benzoin gum. Add two tables- poons of this mixture to two ounces of oil.*

CONFUSION OIL

Use in rituals to confuse an enemy trying to harm you.

> *Mix two parts of rue and one part of guinea pepper. Add two tablespoons of this mixture to two ounces of oil.*

CONTROLLING OIL

Place three drops of this oil on another's shoes. To have better control over a situation or person, write the situation or the person's name on a piece of paper, place the paper under a purple candle dressed with this oil. Burn daily until the candle is consumed and your dominance over the situation or person should be established.

> *Two tablespoons of calamus are added to two ounces of oil.*

CROSSING OIL

Use on candles or charms used in rituals designed to curse another.

> *Mix equal amounts of wormwood and pepperwort. Of this mixture put two tablespoons in two ounces of oil. OPTIONAL: add a small piece of ground-ivy root to each bottle of oil.*

COURAGE OIL

Add nine drops of this oil to the bath water when applying for a job or asking the boss for a raise. As a perfume, anoint on the throat, below the heart and above the naval to replace fears and timidity.

> *Mix equal parts of the following: rosemary, five-finger grass, and gardenia petals. Add two tablespoons of the above mixture to two ounces of oil. Add a small piece of High John the Conqueror root to each bottle of oil made.*

DREAM OIL

Place a few drops on your pillow before going to sleep. Anoint on your forehead, throat and below the heart when used in rituals to bring about prophetic dreams or astral projection.

> *Mix equal parts of grated lemon peel or lemon flowers, frankincense and myrrh.*

*Use two tablespoons of this mixture to
two ounces of oil. OPTIONAL: place a bit of
five-finger grass in each bottle of oil made.*

FRIENDLY JUDGE OIL

Used in dealing with the courts and lawyers. Add to bath
water for three days before court date. As a perfume, anoint
on arms, bosom and throat on the court date. Rub on fingers
before signing any legal papers.

*Mix together two parts of carnation petals,
one part of anise seed and one part of
cinnamon. Use two tablespoons of this
mixture to two ounces of oil. A small
piece of galangal root is added to each
bottle of oil made.*

GAMBLER'S LUCK OIL

Anoint on charms designed to bring luck in gambling. It
can be rubbed on the palms before gambling. Anoint each
corner of your bingo card before the game begins. Anoint in
your shoes before going to the race track.

*Mix together three parts of cinnamon,
one part carnation petals and one part
anise seed. Add two tablespoons of this
mixture to two ounces of oil. Place a
small piece of High John the Conqueror
root in each bottle of oil made.*

GYPSY BLOOD OIL

Said to make a troublesome neighbor uproot and move
when sprinkled on their doorknob.

*Mix two parts of patchouli leaves with
one part of guinea pepper. Use two tablespoons of the above mixture to two
ounces of oil.*

HAPPY HEART OIL

This is an oil said to help attract happiness and many good vibrations.

> *Use two tablespoons of wisteria flowers in two ounces of oil.*

HEALTH ATTRACTING OIL

This oil is usually anointed on the forehead of the ill.

> *Use two tablespoons in two ounces of oil of any one of the following scents; rose, carnation, gardenia, grated lemon peel or lemon flowers.*

HOME PROTECTION OIL

Anointed on charms designed to protect the home from evil. Sprinkled about the home to keep evil influences away.

> *Use equal parts of the following; five-finger grass, sandalwood, gardenia petals and purslane herb. Add two tablespoons of this mixture to two ounces of oil. One pinch of blessed salt is put in each bottle of oil made.*

LOVE DRAWING OIL

Said to help attract a lover. As a perfume anoint on the forehead, heart and genitals.

> *Use two tablespoons of any one of the following: jasmine, red rose or lavender to two ounces of oil. A small piece of orris root is added to each bottle of oil made.*
>
> *—or—*
>
> *Mix together two parts of red rose petals to one part of cinnamon. Use two tablespoons of this mixture to two ounces of oil. A small piece of orris root is added*

to each bottle of oil made.

LUCKY LIFE OIL

Said to be a luck attracting oil. Anoint the money you are using to gamble with this oil. Rub on the palms of your hands before playing cards or throw dice.

> *Mix together two parts of cinnamon and one part of chamomile and one part of peony. Add two tablespoons of this herb mixture to two ounces of oil. OPTIONAL: one tonka bean to each bottle of oil made.*

MISTRESS OF THE HOUSE OIL

This oil is used by women who want to be the boss of the house. Sprinkle on mate or lover's shoes or clothing to gain control over his actions.

> *Add two tablespoons of calamus to two ounces of oil. A small piece of devil's shoestring is added to each bottle of oil made.*

MONEY DRAWING OIL

Anoint inside your wallet or purse daily. It is said your money will return double if anointed on the four corners of your paper money. When applying for a loan, try anointing this oil on the heels of both feet before leaving home.

> *Mix equal parts of the following: frankincense, myrrh and sandalwood. Use two tablespoons of this mixture to two ounces of oil. A bit of bayberry herb is added to each bottle of oil made.*

PEACEFUL HOME OIL

Put nine drops of this oil in a bowl of water and sprinkle in every corner of the home to lessen tension among those who are angry with one another. Dress a white candle with this oil and burn daily with some Circle of Protection Incense.

> *Mix two parts of white rose petals with one part of cumin seed. Two tablespoons of this mixture is added to two ounces of oil.*

PEACEFUL THOUGHTS OIL

This oil is useful in rituals to bring about peaceful thoughts. Anoint on the forehead and temples. Useful when beginning meditation.

> *Use equal parts of the following; lavender, rosemary and wintergreen herbs. Two tablespoons of this mixture is added to two ounces of oil.*

POWER OIL

Said to help increase your own power. Anoint on the forehead, throat, breast bone and above the navel. Useful in any ritual when designed to increase your own power in any situation. Anoint on charms for psychic and spiritual development.

> *Mix together equal parts of grated lemon peel or lemon flowers with frankincense. Add two tablespoons to two ounces of oil.*

PROTECTION OIL

Wear as a perfume. Anoint the forehead, throat and breast bone. Anoint on charms or use in rituals designed to protect from evil.

> *Mix equal parts of sandalwood, patchouli leaves and gardenia petals. Use two tablespoons of the mixture to two ounces of oil. Put a pinch of blessed salt in each*

bottle of oil made.

SEDUCTION OIL

It is said that this oil will help you to seduce anyone you may choose when worn as a perfume. Anoint behind the ears, under the left armpit, in back of the neck and between the thighs.

> *Use two tablespoons of cloves in two ounces of oil. OPTIONAL: Add a small piece of verbena root (said to make passions quickly rise) in each bottle of oil made.*

STRAY NO MORE OIL

Said to keep a lover or mate faithful. Use in a mate's bath water. Anoint on the soles of your mate or lover's shoes. Sprinkle on the bed sheets.

> *Mix together two parts of spikenard, one part of linden flowers and one part of herba mate. Two tablespoons of this mixture is added to two ounces of oil. OPTIONAL: A small piece of magnolia root is put in each bottle of oil made.*

SUCCESS OIL

> *Mix together two parts of sandalwood, five-finger grass and frankincense with one part of cinnamon and one part of grated lemon peel or lemon flowers. Use two tablespoons of this mixture in two ounces of oil. OPTIONAL: Add a small piece of High John the Conqueror root to each bottle of oil made.*

UNCROSSING OIL

> *Mix two parts of sandalwood, patchouli leaves and myrrh, with one part of five-finger grass. Add two tablespoons of this mixture to two ounces of oil. Put a pinch of blessed salt and eight drops of household ammonia to each 1 oz. bottle of oil made. Shake well before each use.*

LOUISIANA VAN VAN OIL

This is an oil much used in the voodoo circles, an oil which has many uses. For uncrossing purposes, add nine drops of the oil to the bath water for nine days daily.

> *Use two tablespoons of lemon grass herb to two ounces of oil. A pinch of blessed salt is added to each bottle of oil made.*

ASTROLOGICAL OILS

These oils are very useful in rituals when astral candles are used to represent individuals. When it comes to using the astral colors in ritual, there is a difference among several authorities as to the color used. Basically, you have a primary color and a secondary color. The famed voodoo queen Marie Laveau listed the astral colors for those born under the sign of Pisces as blue, the primary color; and green, the secondary color. Another authority suggests the astral color for Pisces as pink, the primary color; and green, white or black, a secondary color. Still another authority gives the color white as the primary color for Pisces, and green as the secondary color. In this instance the basic rule is: whichever authority you place the most confidence in, use their colors for the astral candles as well.

In making these oils, use only one herb or flower listed for each of the zodiac signs, following the same technique as given previously.

Aries (March 21 —April 19): Pine, cypress, betony, cowslip, nettles, wormwood, anemone, geranium.

Taurus (April 20—May 20): Musk, rose, carnation, honeysuckle, violet, saffron, burdock, golden rod, mint, periwinkle, primrose, strawberry, vervain, mallow, jasmine, clover.

Gemini (May 21—June 21): Yellow rose, jasmine, bayberry, mastic resin, sandalwood, caraway seed, marjoram, parsley, gladiolus, orchid.

Cancer (June 22—July 22): Aloe, water lily, hyacinth, all nocturnal flowers, bay leaves, larkspur, cedar, myrtle, cinnamon, poppy, blam, daisy, buckbean, sweet flag, sundew, lotus, agrimony.

Leo (July 23—Aug. 22): Red sandalwood, frankincense, camphor, cassia, clove, golden rod, great celandine, eyebright, goat's rue, chamomile flowers, sunflower.

Virgo (August 23—Sept. 22): Morning glory, cornflower, asters, petunias, citron peel, mace, caraway seed, male fern, horehound, lavender, lily, marjoram, snowdrop, narcissus.

Libra (Sept. 23—Oct. 22): Calendula, violet, rose, satinwood, burdock, golden rod, mint, periwinkle, primrose, vervain, pennyroyal, aloe, sandalwood.

Scorpio (Oct. 23—Nov. 21): Chrysanthemum, pine, yucca, rosemary, dogwood, anemone, little calendine, nettles, wormwood, basil, vanilla leaf, cypress.

Sagittarius (Nov. 22—Dec. 21): Daffodil, narcissus, aster, nutmeg, clove, saffron, pimpernel, cinquefoil (five-finger grass), balsam, goat's beard, sage.

Capricorn (Dec. 22—Jan. 19): Frankincense, khus khus, carnation, comfrey, dandelion, Iceland moss, flax seed, thistle, sorrel.

Aquarius (Jan. 20—Feb. 18): Violets, daffodil, pine, pepperwort, sciatica-wort, comfrey, Iceland moss, flax seed, poppy, southernwood, valerian, absinth, fennel, buttercup.

Pisces (Feb. 19—March 20): Lilac, lilies (including water lilies), clove, nutmeg, carnation, cinquefoil, balsam, sage, dock, pellitory, birthwort.

There is an oil called Zodiac Oil which is used to anoint astral candles in ritual. Here we have one oil which can be used for all the zodiac signs, but in this case, when we are dealing with the different signs, it is better to make the particular oil using an herb or flower associated with the zodiac sign or its own planetary ruler.

Once again, use one of the flowers or herbs to make your oil. To make a potent astral candle, simply powder a little bit of another herb given for that sign and mix it in with paraffin of the color for that zodiac sign. Add a wick to it and when the paraffin hardens, you will have a better astral candle.

BASIC ESSENTIAL OILS

If you are using fresh flowers to make your oils, use the flowers gathered after the sun has dried the morning dew from the flowers. The following is a complete list of essential oils you will need according to the recipes in this book. Remember—two tablespoons of the flower or herb to two ounces of oil. If the scent is not as strong as you would like it to be, simply repeat using fresh herb or flowers until you are satisfied.

GARDENIA OIL—use the flower. This is a basic protection oil which will stop others from creating strife in your life.

CINNAMON OIL—use ground cinnamon. Has been used for anointing heads and blessing room where voodoo ceremonies are held. Said to bring good luck. Can be added to scrub waters for extra strength.

PATCHOULI OIL—use the leaves. An oil regarded as an aphrodisiac. Can be used to bring peace of mind, harmony to the home. Said to turn upon the user if used to place a curse on anyone.

JASMINE OIL—use the flowers. This oil is said to attract many good spirits. To bring about good luck and inspire love. Can be substituted for Gardenia Oil.

FRANKINCENSE OIL—use powdered resin. Considered a sacred oil. Sprinkled around the altar and anointed on objects to bring many blessings.

LAVENDER OIL—use the flowers. An oil said to bring complete peace of mind. Said to help inspire love. Causes one to be cautious in all money matters.

RED ROSE OIL—use the petals. A popular oil with voodoo practitioners. Said to attract love.

WHITE ROSE OIL—use the petals. Believed among the voodoo practitioners to bring peace and harmony to one's life. Can be worn as a perfume during times of stress to gain spiritual strength.

SPIKENARD OIL—An oil considered to attract spiritual qualities and blessings. The scent is considered to be long lingering. It is worn as a perfume when meeting those separated by distance. It is felt to bring back warm feelings and fond memories of the past.

MYRRH OIL—use powdered resin. This oil is believed to be a powerful aid to ward off evil and break any hexes directed toward you.

Chapter Eight

SPRINKLING POWDERS

Sprinkling powders have been used in ritual to gain the help of spiritual beings. They are also used in gris-gris bags, as a dusting powder, or sprinkled about the house and on clothing.

In your mortar and pestle, powder all of the solid ingredients and add the liquid ingredients. Once the liquid is completely blended with the herbs, slowly add the talc. Since the talc will not absorb the liquid ingredients, it is always added last. As you combine all the ingredients, chant a rhyme pertaining to the purpose for which the powder is made.

CROSSING POWDER
>1 oz. powdered wormwood
>½ oz. powder pine needles
>¼ oz. graveyard dirt
>1 tbsp. guinea pepper
>1 dram of crossing oil
>4 oz. talc

LOVE DRAWING POWDER
>1 oz. powdered sandalwood
>¼ tsp. cinnamon

1 tsp. sweet basil
1 tsp. myrtle
½ dram frankincense oil
½ dram spikenard oil
1 dram red rose oil
4 oz. talc

GOLD DUST POWDER
(A Gambling Powder)
1 oz. powdered sandalwood
1 tsp. carnation petals
(dried and powdered)
1 tsp. powdered cinnamon
½ dram frankincense oil
½ dram myrrh oil
4 oz. talc

MONEY DRAWING POWDER
1 oz. powdered sandalwood
¼ tsp. powdered cinnamon
1 tbsp. powdered five-finger grass
1 tsp. powdered yellow dock
½ dram frankincense oil
¼ dram patchouli oil
¼ dram myrrh oil
4 oz. talc

UNCROSSING POWDER
1 oz. powdered sandalwood
1¼ tsp. powdered five-finger grass
½ dram uncrossing oil
¼ dram frankincense oil
¼ dram myrrh oil
4 oz. talc

Chapter Nine

WASHES

Wash is a term given for an herb mixture usually steeped in water and used to sprinkle on or wash down the floor of a home, business, mailbox, etc. It is designed to attract or dispel certain influences.

To make a wash, the herbs are steeped in a pint of fresh water. Store the wash in a previously consecrated dark place for three days prior to use. Each evening shake the wash while chanting a rhyme pertaining to the purpose for making the wash. On the fourth day, strain the herbs from the water as you repeat your chant. Also repeat the chant when you use the wash. Make a fresh batch as often as necessary.

BUSINESS DRAWING WASH

If your business has walk-in customers, wash down the entrance floor, the door handle and the aisle, while using your chant. For a mail order business, and if your business brings in checks through the mail, wash down the mailbox inside and out. Once a week use this wash in your scrub water to wash down the floors and walls of your business. never use this wash longer than a week after you first use it; make a fresh batch when necessary. It is said that this wash is good for attracting tenants to an empty apartment or house.

> *Mix 1 ounce of powdered squill root, 1 ounce of powdered yellow dock, ¼ ounce of five-finger grass, 1 tsp. of cinnamon and a tablespoon of blessed salt. Mix well and add two teaspoons of this mixture to 1 pint of fresh water.*

DAY IN COURT WASH

Three days before your scheduled court appearance, make this wash. Put the bottle in a consecrated dark place and chant over it. Continue the chanting each evening and morning. On the morning of the court date, pour this mixture out of your front door where you must walk through it when you leave the house on your way to court. Carry a large piece of High John the Conqueror root in your pocket to the courtroom.

> *To one pint of water add ¼ oz. jalop powder, ¾ oz. of snake head and one teaspoon of blessed salt.*

NOTE: The Day in Court Wash is best when used in conjunction with a ritual to destroy your enemy's power to harm you.

FOUR THIEVES VINEGAR

Four Thieves Vinegar is used as a hexing agent. The name of the person you wish to curse is written on a piece of paper. The paper is soaked in Four Thieves Vinegar. The paper is allowed to dry and then is burned. It is the ashes of this paper you use in your ritual. Four Thieves Vinegar can be sprinkled on an enemy's door step to break up their home.

> *To a gallon of strong cider vinegar add a handful of the following: rosemary, wormwood, lavender, rue, sage, and mint. Add 1 ounce of powdered camphor gum.*

Tightly close the container with the cider vinegar and herbs in it. Place this container in a pan of water and heat until the water begins to boil. Always shake this mixture before heating. Heat daily for 4 days. Strain the herbs from the liquid, bottle and keep tightly closed.

ESSENCE OF LOUISIANA VAN VAN

Used as a sprinkling solution to attract luck and power of all kinds when used full strength. Add to scrub water to wash down the floor and steps of a home or business to get rid of evil.

Put 1½ oz. of Louisiana Van Van Oil in 16 oz. of alcohol. Shake well before each use.

WATER OF NOTRE DAME

Sprinkle about the house to promote peace and tranquility.

Crush 1½ oz. of white rose petals in 16 oz. of spring water. Let the rose petals steep for three days, strain and bottle the liquid for use.

WATER OF MARS or WAR WATER

Water of Mars is used when you wish to create strife. It is sprinkled in the path of your enemy.

Add 1½ oz. of creolin* to 16 oz. of water.

---

*Creolin or Creosote is an oily liquid obtained from the distillation of coal tar, extensively used to preserve wood from decay.

Chapter Ten

LAGNIAPPE

OPENING RITUAL
(Used mostly by those of Catholic Faith)

Approach the altar with the palms of both hands and thumbs against the breastbone. Standing erect in this posture, kneel; then rise and bow your head in front of the altar. Dip your fingers into the Holy Water and make the sign of the cross as you recite the following:

Touch the forehead as you say:

> *In the name of the Father,*
> *Au nom du pere,*

Touch the breastbone as you say:

> *The Son,*
> *le fils,*

Touch the left shoulder and say:

> *The Holy Spirit,*
> *le Saint Esprit,*

Touch the right shoulder and say:

> *Amen.*
> *Si soit-il.* (Lit. So be it)

Place the palms of both hands together again, kneel and sincerely recite Psalm 51:10-12;

Create in me a clean heart, O God;
and renew a steadfast spirit within me.
Cast me not away from Thy presence, and
take not Thy Holy Spirit from me.
Restore to me the joy of Thy salvation, and
uphold me with a willing spirit:

This ritual uses three altar candles representing God the Father, the Son, and the Holy Spirit.

Altar Candle 1   Altar Candle   Altar Candle 3
2
Angelic Candles (Day candles)
1 2 3 4 5 6 7

1. Light Altar Candle #1 as you recite the following:
   Blessed be God the Father, whom by His
   almighty power and love, created me,making
   all mankind in the Divine image and likeness
   of God.
2. Light Altar Candle #2 as you recite the following:
   Blessed be the Son, Jesus Christ, God's love
   made flesh on earth, who came from the
   Father to show us the path leading into the
   Kingdom of Heaven and life everlasting among
   all saints.
3. Light Altar Candle #3 as you say:
   Blessed be the Holy Spirit, sent to us by the
   grace of the Father as promised by Jesus of
   Nazareth, sanctifying me and will continue to
   sanctify all of God's children.
4. Light the Angelic (Day) Candle from the flame of the Holy Spirit candle as you sing/chant the following:

Blessed be God's Holy Angel/Archangel
____*(name)*____, *whom through the will of*
the Father can aid us in our lives. For He shall
give His angels charge over thee,
to keep thee in all thy ways. (Palm 91:11)
Who maketh His angels spirits; His ministers
a flaming fire (Psalm 104:4)

5. Place both palms of your hands together and bow your head as you recite the 'Glory Be':

   Glory be to the Father, and to the Son, and to
   the Holy Spirit, as it was in the beginning, is
   now and ever shall be, world without end.
   Amen.

6. Light incense. As this is done and the smoke rises, chant the following:

   Blessed be God the Eternal, now forever.

7. Pick up the bowl of Holy Water and sprinkle every corner of the room in a clockwise direction. Sprinkle some of the Holy Water to the right of the altar, to the left of the altar, then directly in front of the altar. Recite Psalm 91 — traditionally used for protection in all kinds of danger in life, such as harm from fire or water, murders, robbers, wars, enemies, incurable diseases, prison confinement, plagues, contagious diseases, or prayed over a person who is bothered by negative influences.

   He that dwelleth in the secret place of the
   most High shall abide under the shadow of
   the Almighty.
   I will say of the Lord, he is my refuge and my
   fortress: my God; in Him will I trust.
   Surely He shall deliver thee from the snare of
   the bird catcher, and from vain gossip.
   He shall cover you with His feathers, and
   under His wings shall you trust: His truth
   shall be your shield and buckler.

Nor for the pestilence that walks in darkness;
Nor for the destruction that wastes at noonday.
A thousand will fall at your side, and ten
thousand at your right hand; but it shall not
come near you.
Only with your eyes shall you behold and
see the reward of the wicked.
Because you have made the Lord, which is thy
refuge, even the most High thy habitation.
There will be no evil to befall thee, neither will
any plague come near your dwelling.
For He will give His angels charge over you,
to keep you in all your ways.
They will bear you up in their hands, lest you
dash your foot against a stone.
Thou will tread upon the lion and adder: the
young lion and the great serpent shalt you
trample under feet.
Because He has set His love upon me, and I
will answer Him; I will be with Him in trouble;
I will deliver Him, and show Him my salvation.

8. At this point in the ritual added some more incense, and
as you do this say:
    I burn this incense in this fire as a gesture of
    homage to Thee O Lord.
Take up the incense burner (preferably one with a
chain) and swing it three times toward the altar.
Then in a clockwise direction, circle the room.
Return in front the altar and swing the censor three
times toward the east as you say:
    In honor to you, Raphael (east)
Face south and swing the censor three times as you
say:
    In honor to you, Michael. (south)
Face west and swing the censor three times as

you say:

> *In honor to you, Gabriel.* (west)

Face the north and swing the censor three times as you say:

> *In honor to you, Uriel.* (north)

9. Place the incense burner back on the altar, then recite Psalm 104, keeping in mind that all things and blessings come from God who created all that is in the world. This Psalm is also said to prevent from harm persons, spirits and animals, and to curb the desire to do wrong.

> *Bless the Lord, O my soul: O Lord my God, Thou art very great: Thou are clothed with honor and majesty.*
>
> *Thyself covering with light as with a robe, and stretching out the skies like a tent.*
>
> *He lays the beams of His upper chambers in the waters, the clouds He uses for His chariot, He walks on the wings of the wind.*
>
> *Making the angels His messengers, His ministers like flames of fire.*
>
> *He established the earth on Its foundation, so that it should never be overthrown.*
>
> *Thou did O Lord cover it with the ocean depth for a garment. Above the mountains stood the waters,*
>
> *which surged in retreat at Thy rebuke, at Thy thunderous commandment swirled away,*
>
> *while the mountains sprang up and the valleys descended to the place which Thou did set for them.*
>
> *Thou has set a boundary which the waters cannot pass; the waters will never return to cover the earth.*
>
> *He causes the springs to gush forth into the valleys; which wind their way down through*

the hills.
The waters provide drink for every animal of
the field; the wild donkeys quench their thirst.
The birds of the air make their nests beside
them; they sing among the branches.
He makes the grass to grow for the cattle, fruits
and vegetables for man to cultivate, that he
may bring forth food from the land,
wine to elate the heart of man, oil to brighten
his face, and bread to strengthen man's heart.
The trees of the Lord are full of sap, the cedars
of Lebanon which He had planted.
The birds build their nests in them, and the fir
tree is the stork's home.
He made the high mountain for the wild goats,
the rocks for the badger's refuge.
He made the moon to mark out the seasons;
the sun knows the time for setting.
Thou makes darkness and it is night, so that
all forest animals may roam about.
The young lions roam after their prey and
seek their meat from God.
When the sun comes up, they go back and lie
down in their dens.
Then man comes forth to begin his work and
continues his labor until evening.
O Lord how manifold are your works! In wisdom Thou has made them all. The earth is full
of Thy rich creations.
So is the sea vast and broad; within it things
creeping too many to number, both small
and great beasts.
There go the ships that sail the sea; there's the
leviathan, Thou has made to play within.
All these wait upon Thee O Lord, to give them
their food in due season.
When Thou provides for them, they gather it

in. Thou opens Thy hand,
they are satisfied with good.
When Thou hides Thy face, they are struck
with trouble. When Thou cuts off their breath,
they die and return to their dust.
Thou sends forth Thy Spirit and more are
created, Thou renews the face of the earth.
May the glory of the Lord endure for ever.
May the Lord be pleased with all his works.
He looks on the earth, and it trembles, He
touches the mountains and they smoke.
I will sing to the Lord as long as I live; I will
praise the Lord while I have my being.
May my meditation of the Lord be sweet; I
will be glad in the Lord.
Let the sinners perish from the face of the
earth, and let the ungodly be no more. Bless
thou the Lord, O my soul.
Hallelujah!

Place some more incense to burn, then meditate a few minutes
on the purpose behind doing the ritual.
Go on to doing the ritual intention, be it for financial blessings,
health, to settle disturbed conditions, an uncrossing, etc.

Angelic (Day) Candles

1. **Michael** or Saint Michael; his ruling planet is the sun.
   Michael is represented by an orange candle. He is great
   in power and intelligence. The final arbiter in things. He is
   capable of immense warmth and generosity, or of frighten-
   ing wrath.
2. **Gabriel** or Saint Gabriel; ruling planet, the moon. Has
   strength and grace, but also capable of inconstancy.
   Associated with death, the covert and fickleness of whim.
   Gabriel is represented by a white candle.
3. **Madimiel** governs the planet Mars. Madimiel comes on
   with vehemence, zeal, and driving energy with an ever

present tendency to excess. His great constructive force may go to extreme and become destructive force. A red candle.

4. **Zedekiel** rules the planet Jupiter. Zedekiel is represented by a purple candle. Righteousness, justice, integrity, and fairness are his characteristics.

5. **Raphael** or Saint Raphael, ruler of the planet Mercury. His major characteristics are Intelligence, volatility, the ability to communicate and deal, a tendency to gossip, mathematics, and a talent for financial gain. Raphael should be represented by a yellow candle.

6. **Haniel** is the ruler of Venus. The characteristics of Haniel are peace, light and beauty, kindliness, sensualness and at times self-indulgence. Haniel is symbolized by a green candle.

7. Zophikiel governs Saturn. This angel is represented by a dark blue (preferably) or black candle. Zophikiel's characteristics are as follows: the inevitable, the infinate, secrecies, and mysteries. Zophikiel is the middle-ground between time and eternity, and can bring disasters.
   The archangels in the above list are Michael, Gabriel, and Raphael; the rest are simply angels. Uriel is also an archangel, and his name means 'Light of God'. Uriel is the archangel ruling the northern quarters, and his color is green.

Closing the Ritual

1. Extinguish all candles you used in relation to your ritual intention, in reverse order. Only the Altar Candles and the Angelic Candle should be left to burn.

2. If needed, put some more incense to burn.

3. Recite Psalm 150:
   Praise ye the Lord. Praise God in His sanctu ary;
   Praise Him in the firmament of His mighty power.

*Praise Him for His mighty deeds; praise Him
according to His excellent greatness.
Praise Him with the sound of the trumpet;
praise Him with the psaltery and harp.
Praise Him with the timbrel and dance;
praise Him with stringed instruments and
organs.
Praise Him upon the loud cymbals; praise
Him upon the high sounding cymbals.
Let every thing that has breath praise the
Lord. Hallelujiah.*

4. Extinguish the Angelic/Day Candle, while thanking the angel in your own words for any assistance with the problem at hand.

5. Before extinguishing the Altar Candles, recite the following prayer:

   *As the Father knows me, so may I know the
   Father, through Christ Jesus, the door to the
   kingdom of the Father, show Thou me the
   way.*

   Place the palms of both hands together with the thumbs against the breastbone, and kneel and bow your head. Rise and extinguish the Altar Candles in the reverse order of lighting them.

A Candlelight Service

This service is done at night using mostly the Psalms from the Bible. This type of religious service is designed for a group of people coming together in prayer. One person is needed to conduct and lead the service. A male or female can be the leader in this service, and will be referred to as leader throughout.

Before beginning the service, it is necessary to have the correct number of seven day novena candles (these are candles in clear glass), one for each person attending the candlelight service. One colored candle, depending on the need for the candlelight service, will be lit by the leader only.

The leader will perform steps 1 through 7 as outlined in the Opening Ritual (used mostly by those of Christian faith).

8. Place some more incense in the burner, and take up the bowl of Holy Water. Walking in a clockwise direction, make the sign of the cross on the forehead of each person present for the service, giving the following benediction:

> May this Holy Water cleanse you in mind, body and spirit. In the name of the Father, Son, and Holy Spirit, that God may judge you worthy to receive His blessings.

When finished, return the Holy Water back to the altar.

9. The leader will now hand each person one seven day novena candle. After everyone has their candle, the leader will then pour a few drops of anointing oil on top of the seven day novena candles, asking each person to rub the oil in a clockwise direction while concentrating on their prayer.

10. As the other people are concentrating on their prayer, the Leader will turn to the altar and recite Psalm 21:

> The king shall joy in Thy strength
> O Lord; and in Thy salvation how
> greatly shall he rejoice!
> Thou has given him his heart's desire, and
> has not withheld the request of his lips.
> For thou do meet him with blessings of goodness; Thou do place a crown of pure gold on
> his head.
> He asked life of Thee; Thou gave it to him;
> even length of days forever and ever.

His glory is great because of Thy deliverance; honor and majesty Thou does bestow upon him.

Yes, forever Thou does make his most blest; Thou does delight him with joy of Thy presence.

For the king trusts in the Lord; and because the covenant love of the Most High he shall not be moved.

Your hand will find out all your enemies; your right hand will find out those who hate you.

You will make them like a blazing furnace when you appear; the Lord will swallow them up in His anger, and fire will devour them.

You will destroy their offspring from the earth and their children from the sons of men.

For they have intended evil against you; they have devised a plot; they will be unable to put into practice.

For you will make them turn their backs; you will aim at their faces with your bows.

Be Thou exalted, O Lord, in Thy strength; we will sing and praise Thy power.

11. The Leader will then light the colored candle from the already burning Angelic/Day Candle, (refer to the list of colors and their vibratory meanings) symbolizing the purpose for the candlelight service. Each person will then, one at a time, approach the altar and light their seven day candle using a taper from the flame of the colored candle. The seven day novena candles are placed in a semi-circle around the colored candle, which is placed in the center of the Altar.

12. Once all present have lit their candles and have returned to their seats, the leader will kneel in front of the altar and begin to chant the Psalm appropriate for the candlelight

service. It is important for the leader to chant slowly, so that each person can repeat the Psalm after him/her. The Psalm is chanted in this manner three times.

13. Be sure to close the Novena Candlelight Service using the closing ritual with Psalm 150 before anyone is allowed to leave the premises.

14. This brings to an end the Novena Candlelight Service. All who participated in the service must daily recite the Psalm for seven days.

The colored candle is allowed to burn for one hour, and is then extinguished by the leader. The other novena candles are allowed to remain burning until they extinguish themselves. However, the colored candle is relit each day as the leader recites the Psalm pertaining to the candlelight service, and is allowed to burn one hour. This is continued for seven days. On the last day the colored candle is allowed to burn itself out.

USING THE PSALMS FOR SOLVING PROBLEMS

For years the Psalms have been used with surprising results for helping to solve many of the problems that arise from daily living. The following list will aid you in deciding which Psalm to use for your problem.

For a person who wishes greater spiritual awareness—Psalm 99.

Before moving into a new home for luck and blessings—Psalm 61.

For all your undertakings to be fortunate and advantageous—Psalm 65.

To have good luck in all you do—Psalm 57.

To change an unhappy situation into a happy one—Psalm 16.

So daily needs can be obtained and avoid harm—Psalm 77.

To rid yourself of strong negative influences—Psalm 19.

To release from the heart deep seated hate, envy and spite—Psalm 137.

For defense against enemies, rivals and assailants—Psalms 3,; 59; 70.

For illness or bad health—Psalm 23; 35; 38.

For thanksgiving or recovery from illness—Psalm 30.

To bring peace or blessings to the home—Psalm 1; 128.

For spiritual support in stress or affliction—Psalm 3; 25; 54.

To bring harmony between people or groups—Psalm 133.

To petition for material needs (money, food, clothing, etc.) Psalm 41.

For trouble by slander—Psalm 38; 39.

To receive grace, love and mercy—Psalm 32.

To be respected and loved by others—Psalm 47.

To protect against unjust slander—Psalm 36.

So idle gossip will not harm you or cause agitation—Psalm 36.

For protection from an enemy who will not leave you alone—Psalm 109.

To free yourself from harmful or evil habits—Psalm 69.

To reconcile with an enemy—Psalm 16.

To overcome an enemy in a just manner—Psalm 70.

To have more friends—Psalm 111.

To keep the love of friends and acquire more friends—Psalm 133.

To bring peace and harmony between families—Psalm 98.

To do good and avoid evil—Psalm 87.

To cast out evil influences from another—Psalm 29.

For someone in prison to be released early—Psalm 26.

To be safe from any planned robberies or danger—Psalm 50.

For safety if traveling alone at night—Psalm 122.

For a safe ending in your travels—Psalm 34.

To be accepted, liked and respected by all—Psalm 47.

To remove negative influences you feel around yourself—
Psalm 10.

To win a lawsuit if opposed by an unjust or revengeful person—
Psalm 35.

If appearing before a judge and want a favorable verdict—
Psalm 20.

To receive justice and a favorable hearing from a lawsuit—
Psalm 119, Lamed.

For anyone who drinks too much—Psalm 87.

If the law is taking measures to punish you—Psalm 35.

For reconciling between man and wife—Psalm 45; 46.

For possession by an evil spirit—Psalm 66.

To revenge yourself from secret enemies—Psalm 53-55.

If enemies caused you to lose money and be mistrusted—
Psalm 41, 43, (3 times daily for 3 days with appropriate
prayer to your situation)

To overcome trouble and loss from business partners—
Psalm 63.

To make your home lucky—Psalm 61.

To receive Holy Blessings—Psalm 62.

When using the Psalms, it is important to softly sound the words so that the vibrations gently fall or vibrate upon your ears. If you can chant the Psalm in this soft tone, so much the better. At the end of the Psalm, imagine/petition your desire with as few words as possible.

PRAYERS TO THE SAINTS

In Louisiana and all areas of the New World where Hoodoo is a practice, many of the old Voodoo gods (though they are not gods but are called Lois—a French word meaning laws) were replaced by the Catholic Saints. Invoking the Saints for help in life's problems in my opinion is not that much different from European and African polytheism. The function of the

Saints has blended in quite well in representing the different African gods and goddesses in the Voodoo practices in Haiti, and the Macumba cults in Brazil today.

The various Saints are traditionally invoked as follows:

The Guardian Angel—for protection.

Our Lady of Lourdes—for healing the sick.

Our Lady of Perpetual Help—for assistance in all things.

The Sacred Heart of Jesus—for daily blessings.

Saint Anne the Mother of Mary—for grandmothers, friendship and love.

St. Anthony—success in all things, regain a lost lover, to get back lost or stolen things.

St. Barbara—for courage and protection.

St. Basil—for justice in all legal matters.

St. Bernard—for special favors.

St. Raphael the Archangel—for good travel.

St. Christopher—for safety in travel.

St. Clara—for understanding in all matters.

St. Cyril—for daily needs and blessings.

St. Dymphna—on behalf of those with mental or nervous illness.

St. Elena—to overcome sorrow and sadness.

St. Expedite—for quick help in your pressing need.

St. Francis of Assisi—for serenity and spiritual blessings.

St. Gerard Maiella—for motherhood and expectant mothers.

St. Joan of Arc—for courage and victory.

St. Joseph—for family blessings and work.

St. Lucy—to be free from all evil and wickedness.

St. Lazarus (Patron Saint of the poor)—for daily needs.

St. Jude (Patron Saint of the impossible)—help with difficult matters.

St. Martin de Porres—for spiritual development, psychic healing, freedom from sin.

St. Michael the Archangel—courage, protection, and deliverance from enemies and the forces of evil.

St. Mary Magdalene—for self-improvement.
St. Peter—for spiritual growth and mercy from God.
St. Raymond and/or The Holy Family—for peace, love within
the family.
St. Theresa—for humility and spirituality.
St. Mary, Mother of God—for health, daily help, and when in
need of forgiveness.

PRAYER TO SAINT JOSEPH

Saint Joseph, father and guardian of virgins,
into whose faithful keeping were entrusted
Innocency itself, Jesus Christ, and Mary, the
Virgin of virgins, I pray and beseech thee through
Jesus and Mary to intercede on my behalf to
God the Father.
(HERE MAKE YOUR REQUEST FOR HELP)
May I go about my daily work with faithfulness,
honesty, and gladness of heart, helping me to
take your example to provide for those who
depend upon me. Keep me from all uncleanli-
ness, and to grant that my mind be untainted,
my heart pure and my body chaste; help me to
serve our Lord Jesus in all daily works.

Amen

PRAYER TO SAINT GERADO MAIELLA
(A prayer for motherhood)

O good Saint Gerard, powerful intercessor
before God and wonder-worker of our day, I
call upon thee and seek thy aid. Intercede
before God on my behalf that I may have the

love, patience, and true understanding to raise up my children to God. Thou who on earth did always fulfill God's design, help me, I ask with true humility and firm assurance of your help. Beseech the Master of Life, from Whom all paternity proceeds to render me fruitful in my responsibility to teach my children Godly character in this life and heirs to the Kingdom of God and His glory in the world to come.

Amen.

PRAYER TO ST. JUDE

(Many practitioners have told me that St. Jude will grant your wish, but he will also keep you in a bind so that you will constantly pray to him.)

St. Jude, glorious Apostle, faithful servant and friend of Jesus, the name of the person has caused you to be forgotten by many, but you are invoked as the patron of hopeless cases and things despaired of; pray for me, that finally I may receive the consolations and the succor of Heaven in all my necessities, tribulations and sufferings, particularly,
(HERE MAKE YOUR REQUEST FOR HELP)
and that I may bless God with the Elect throughout Eternity. I promise to spread your name with love and compassion for the granting of my request from this day forward. I know you will not fail me, and that joy and happiness will follow me during this difficult time.

Amen

PRAYER TO SAINT DYMPHNA
(On behalf of those with mental or nervous illness)

Lord Jesus Christ, You have willed that St. Dymphna should be invoked by thousands of clients as the patroness of nervous and mental disease, and have brought it about that her interest in these patients should be an inspiration to and an ideal of charity throughout the world. Grant that, through the prayers of this youthful martyr of purity, those who suffer from nervous and mental illness everywhere on earth may be helped and consoled. I recommend to You in particular ... (HERE NAME THOSE YOU WISH TO PRAY FOR) ...

Be pleased to hear the prayers of St. Dymphna and of your Blessed Mother, Health of the sick and Comforter of the afflicted, on behalf of those whom I recommend to the love and compassion of Your Sacred Heart. Give them patience to bear with their affliction and resignation to do Your divine will. Give them the consolation they need and especially the cure they so much desire, if it be Your will. may we all serve Your suffering members with a charity which may merit for us the reward of being united forever in Heaven, who live and reign with the Father in the unity of the Holy Spirit forever,

Amen

PRAYER TO OUR MOTHER OF PERPETUAL HELP

O Mother of Perpetual Help, grant that I may ever invoke Thy must powerful name, which is the safeguard of the living and the salvation of

the dying, O Purest Mary, O Sweetest Mary, let Thy name henceforth be ever on my lips. Delay not, O Blessed Lady, to help me whenever I call on Thee, for, in all my needs,
(AGAIN MAKE YOUR REQUEST FOR HELP)
in all my temptations I shall never cease to call on Thee, ever repeating Thy sacred name, Mary, Mary.
(AGAIN MAKE YOUR REQUEST FOR HELP)
O what consolation, what sweetness, what confidence, what emotion fills my soul when I pronounce Thy sacred name, or even only think of Thee. I thank God for having given Thee, for my good, so sweet, so powerful, so lovely a name. But I will not be content with merely pronouncing Thy name: let my love for Thee prompt me ever to hail Thee, Mother of Perpetual Help. Amen.
(RECITE NINE HAIL MARYS)

PRAYER TO THE INFANT JESUS
OF PRAGUE

O Jesus, Who has said, ask and you shall receive, seek and you shall find, knock and it shall be opened to you, through the intercession of Mary, Thy Most Holy Mother. I knock, I seek, I ask that my prayer be granted.
(HERE MAKE YOUR REQUEST FOR FAVOR)
Oh Jesus, Who has said, all that you ask of the Father in My Name, He will grant to you. Guide me with the Holy Spirit that I may bless you always for what you have done. I humbly and urgently ask Thy Father in Thy Name that my

prayer be granted.
(HERE MAKE YOUR REQUEST FOR FAVOR)
Oh Jesus, Who has said, "Heaven and earth shall pass away but My word shall not pass", I feel confident that my prayer will be granted. You have fortified me on every side by providing for my needs. I come to you with thanksgiving. Amen.

PRAYER TO THE SACRED HEART OF JESUS

O God, Who dost deign mercifully to bestow upon us infinite treasures of love in the Heart of Thy Son, Jesus, who was pierced by our sins and broken hearted by our ingratitude, grant I beseech Thee, that I may pay Him the devout homage of my piety, and clarity of mind, a healthy body, and a peaceful soul so that I can go about my daily tasks with compassion and tranquility and serenity of spirit. Keep me this day constantly before thy eye because in Thee I put my trust. May I learn to walk in the footsteps of your beloved Son, Jesus, that I may be worthy to receive Your blessing in my situation. (HERE NAME YOUR REQUEST FOR HELP) Through the same Christ our Lord. Amen.

PRAYER TO SAINT MICHAEL

Please protect us, St. Michael the Archangel, against violence, murder and robbery. In your goodness, preserve us today from all the malice of sinful and wicked men. In your sleepless vigilance, watch over the safety and welfare of our homes, and keep guard over our possessions. Ever hold in your special care, most triumphant Saint Michael, the forces of public order against the crimes of evil men, and defend all honest citizens in time of peril. We ask this of you through Jesus Christ, our Lord. For the Lord God has given your angels charge of us, to keep us in all our ways.

(HERE STATE THE AREA IN WHICH PROTECTION IS MOST NEEDED AT THIS TIME)

Saint Michael, Archangel of God, defend us in battle and protect us against the wickedness and snares of the devil.

May God rebuke Satan, we humbly pray, and by God's power may you, Prince of the heavenly host, cast him into Hell with all the evil spirits who wander through the world for the ruin of souls.

PRAYER TO SAINT EXPEDITE

St. Expedite, you lay in rest. I come to you and ask that this wish be granted.

(HERE NAME YOUR WISH OR DESIRE)

Expedite this, what I ask of you. Expedite now this I want of you, this very second. Don't waste another day. Give me what I ask for. I know your power, I know you because of your work. I know you can do it. You do this for me and I'll spread your name with love and honor. Expedite this wish with speed, love, honor and goodness. My Glory to you, saint Expedite!

Saint Expedite is said to be a good worker in matters when quick help is needed. Best when used in connection with a quick help lamp.

PRAYER TO SAINT ANNE

O Glorious St. Anne, filled with compassion for those who invoke thee, and love for those who suffer, heavily laden with the weight of my troubles, I cast myself at thy feet and humbly beg of thee to take the present affair which I recommend to thee under thy special protection.
(HERE MAKE YOUR REQUEST FOR OBTAINING THE SPECIAL FAVOR)
Vouchsafe to recommend it to thy Daughter, the Blessed Virgin Mary, and lay it before the throne of Jesus, so that He may bring it to a happy issue. Cease not to intercede for me until my request is granted (REPEAT REQUEST). Above all, obtain for me the grace of one day beholding my God face to face, and with thee and Mary and all the Saints, praising and blessing Him to all eternity.

May I be brave in peril, constant in tribulation, temperate in wrath, and serene in all changes of life, that I may be loyal and loving to all those with whom I come in contact daily.

Good Saint Anne, mother of her who is our Life, our Sweetness and our Hope, pray to her for us, and obtain our request.
(REPEAT THREE TIMES DAILY)

PRAYER TO SAINT ANTHONY

O Holy St. Anthony, the gentlest of Saints, your love for God and charity for His creatures have made you worthy, when on earth, to possess miraculous powers. Miracles waited on your word, which you were ever ready to speak for those in trouble or anxiety. Encouraged by this thought, I implore of you to help obtain for me (HERE STATE YOUR REQUEST OR DESIRE FOR HELP.) The answer to my prayer may require a miracle, even so, you are the Saint of Miracles. O gentle and loving St. Anthony, whose heart was ever full of human sympathy, whisper my petition into the ears of the Holy Infant Jesus, who loved to be held in your arms; and the gratitude of my heart will ever be yours. Amen.

When praying to Saint Anthony for his help, it is best to burn a brown candle daily until request is granted.

Saint Anthony is also good for bringing back a strayed lover. The procedure is taught as follows:

Go out in your yard, be sure no one is looking, and cup your hand to your mouth like a megaphone. Call the person's name three times using equal stressed syllables, then ask Saint Anthony to bring back the person, Call the person's name again telling them St. Anthony is bringing them back which they can't resist. Ask St. Anthony again to bring back that person. Do this three times facing north, east, south and west. Go inside your home and wait for the named person to return.

PRAYER TO SAINT ANTHONY

(For the return of lost or stolen goods if not thrown in water. It is believed that once the stolen item is thrown in water, there is no hope of getting it back. Traditional) We call this prayer the *roulaison*. To begin the prayer, it is necessary to have a picture of Saint Anthony placed at the head of your bed. The Roulaison is repeated over and over, keeping the lost or stolen item in mind until you fall asleep. The prayer is as follows:

> La roulaison, Saint Antoine de Padue qui t'invoque, que ton besoin involve de père et mere est commitier de prepier entre le férmetier. Père pour empêche le médier au mort subite. Qui nous fait recouvrir toute chose perdu. Qui nous fait gagner le process content. Jeune et vieux, qu'on voir encore devant le roi de tout le monde, au repose directé.

CAUTION: There are some practitioners who will not do the Roulaison for the return of lost or stolen items. I have been informed personally from other practitioners that when they do the Roulaison, they experience nightmares or exhaustion from lack of sleep because they are not able to fall asleep. Personally I have not experienced this when I do the Roulaison.

PRAYER TO SAINT THERESA
(For humility and spirituality)

O Lord, who has said: "Unless you become as little children, you shall not enter into the kingdom of heaven"; grant us, we beseech Thee, so to walk in the footsteps of thy blessed Virgin Theresa with a humble and single heart, that we may attain to everlasting rewards: who lives and reigns world without end. I earnestly pray for help, knowing that my vanity, my pride, and my arrogance are keeping me from knowing the love of God. Take from me these base instincts which cause me to wander from my spiritual goal to know God in my daily life. Amen.

PRAYER TO SAINT CHRISTOPHER
(A traveler's prayer)

Though St. Christopher was fired from his job in the early seventies and is no longer a saint, people still pray to him for protection while traveling.

Grant me O Lord a steady hand and
a watchful eye.
That no one shall be hurt as I pass
by.
Thou gavest life, I pray no act of
mine.
May take away or mar that gift of
Thine.
Shelter those, dear Lord, who bear
me company,
From the evils of fire and all
calamity.
Teach me to use my car for others'
needs;
Nor miss through love of undue
speed.
The beauty of the world; that thus
I may
With joy and courtesy go on my way.
St. Christopher, holy patron of
travelers,
Protect me and lead me safely to my destiny.

PRAYER TO SAINT DOMINIC

O holy Priest of God and glorious Patriarch, Saint Dominic, thou who was the friend, the well-loved son and confidant of the Queen of Heaven, and did work so many miracles by the power of the Holy Rosary, have regard for my necessities.
(MAKE YOUR REQUEST HERE)
On earth you opened your heart to the mysteries of your fellow men and your hands were strong to help them; now in heaven your charity has not grown less, nor has your power waned. Pray for me to the Mother of the Rosary and to her divine Son,
(AGAIN MAKE YOUR REQUEST)
for I have great confidence that through your assistance I shall obtain the favor I so much desire. Amen.
PRAY THE ROSARY

Saint Dominique is prayed to help in acquiring your daily needs and blessings.

Conclusion

BEING A PRACTITIONER

In being a practitioner you will come to realize that all the charms you make, all the rituals you do will be like a double-edged sword that cuts both ways. The energy created will reach its mark and eventually return to its source, you, its originator. This is one of the interrelated principles of energy, the Law of Radiation and Attraction. Because of this law we always reap what we sow. As long as you always strive to use your magick to help and benefit others, you will be helping yourself at the same time.

At times a practitioner's life can be difficult, especially when a client waits until the last minute to get help in their situation, expecting you to work a miracle for them overnight. Some clients will exaggerate as they explain their situation to import a need for urgency. There may be other practitioners in your area who will try to discredit your abilities to the public. Normally, these are the ones who create smoke screens to hide the fact that they are only using the occult to make a fast buck. A sincere practitioner can harmoniously and peacefully coexist in an area with other practitioners simply because a sincere practitioner realizes the fact that he/she cannot satisfactorily benefit and aid a town of twenty thousand people or more alone. In the town where I presently live, there are

161

five practitioners that I know of.

There are two things that being a practitioner will bring into your life. The admiration and respect from the people of your community, or ridicule and unnecessary harassment. All of this depends on you, on how you conduct yourself in your public and private life. It is not advisable to dress in a weird fashion or to flaunt the fact that you practice magick. This type of action will bring you ridicule in a hurry. If you use your magickal knowledge to strike fear in the hearts of people or say that you will put a curse of some sort on them if they don't jump to your every whim, you will experience hatred. People quickly learn to hate the thing or person they fear. On the other hand, a wise practitioner lives as normal a life as possible. He/she is always honest and exhibits right moral conduct in dealings with all people. A wise practitioner does not judge other people's lifestyles, but learns to see all people on a spiritual level. It is on this level that a wise practitioner meets and deals with all individuals equally. Is only through this type of conduct that a practitioner earns the trust and respect of the people in the community he/she serves. A wise practitioner never discusses the ritual work presently being done. He/she never reveals to clients who their other clients may be, or the nature of any work which was done for them. If you boast in front of a client, you risk losing that client's trust. People who come to you arrive with the understanding that any work you do for them will be held in the utmost confidence. Therefore, you must impress upon your client that they should not discuss the work you are doing for them to anyone. People will talk, and if the client discusses it with another, he/she should tell you as soon as possible. This way you will free yourself from being blamed for any gossip which may occur about the client or the nature of the work you've done for them.

There will be times when someone will come to you wanting you to break up a love affair for them. I always refuse to do this type of work. I firmly believe it wrong to use magick to interfere in a person's life without their permission. Experience has taught me that these people who are quick to break up a love affair usually have selfish or possessive motives. In this type of a situation I offer to do work to help that person meet someone else who may be more compatible to them.

If you decide to go public, it would be best to make yourself available for consultation only so many hours during the day and perhaps certain days of the week. If not, you may find yourself having people come to your home at three or four in the morning wanting to have work done for them. This happens often to practitioners who keep the open door policy. Some people tend to believe that when a person does this type of service for the community, they should be on call twenty-four hours a day, and have no right to any private, personal life.

Always try to get your client to work with you is the ritual, e.g. have him/her take a ritual bath daily. This helps to set a certain vibration within the individual's aura. Also, have the client burn candles while taking the bath. The color of the candle will depend upon the goals to be achieved through ritual. Most practitioners will have their client burn nine candles, one for each day. A few practitioners will help their client construct a magick lamp to use instead of candles.

Whenever you decide to compose a new spell or charm, use it on yourself first. Never use another as the guinea pig in your magick. If any adverse effects occurred in that person's life, you will be held accountable.

In leaving, I recommend the following books as worthwhile reading, especially for beginners:

1. *Practical Candleburning Rituals* by Raymond Buckland (Llewellyn)
2. *Practical Color Magick* by Raymond Buckland (Llewellyn)
3. *Magical Herbalism—the Secret Craft of the Wise* by

Scott Cunningham (Llewellyn)
4. *The Llewellyn Practical Guide to Creative Visualization* by Melita Denning & Osborne Phillips (Llewellyn)
5. *Helping Yourself With White Witchcraft* by Al Manning (Prentice-Hall)

SUPPLY SOURCE

If there is no occult shop within your area, the following mail order companies would send you a copy of their latest catalog if you write to them.

Tyrad Co.
Box 17006
Minneapolis, MN 55417
send $1.00, by airmail $2.00

International Imports
Box 2010
Toluca Lake, CA 91620
send $2.00

The Occult Emporium
102 North 9th Street
Allentown, PA 18102
send $1.50

Astrology & Spiritual Publishers
4535 Hohman Avenue
Hammond, IN 46327
send $1.00 postage

Hermetic Sanctum
Box 251
Beloit, WI 53511
send $1.00

Tenzing Momo
93 Pike St.
Seattle, WA 98108
Phone: (206) 623-9837

INDEX

STAY IN TOUCH

On the following pages you will find some of the books now available on related subjects. Your book dealer stocks most of these and will stock new titles in the Llewellyn series as they become available. We urge your patronage.

To obtain our full catalog, to keep informed about new titles as they are released and to benefit from informative articles and helpful news, you are invited to write for our bimonthly news magazine/catalog, *Llewellyn's New Worlds of Mind and Spirit*. A sample copy is free, and it will continue coming to you at no cost as long as you are an active mail customer. Or you may subscribe for just $10.00 in the U.S.A. and Canada ($20.00 overseas, first class mail). Many bookstores also have *New Worlds* available to their customers. Ask for it.

Llewellyn's New Worlds of Mind and Spirit
P.O. Box 64383-L501, St. Paul, MN 55164-0383, U.S.A.

* * *

TO ORDER BOOKS AND TAPES

If your book dealer does not have the books described, you may order them directly from the publisher by sending full price in U.S. funds, plus $3.00 for postage and handling for orders *under* $10.00; $4.00 for orders *over* $10.00. There are no postage and handling charges for orders over $50.00. Postage and handling rates are subject to change. We ship UPS whenever possible. Delivery guaranteed. Provide your street address as UPS does not deliver to P.O. Boxes. Allow 4-6 weeks for delivery. UPS to Canada requires a $50.00 minimum order. Orders outside the U.S.A. and Canada: Airmail—add retail price of book; add $5.00 for each non-book item (tapes, etc.); add $1.00 per item for surface mail.

FOR GROUP STUDY AND PURCHASE

Because there is a great deal of interest in group discussion and study of the subject matter of this book, we offer a special quantity price to group leaders or agents. Our special quantity price for a minimum order of five copies of *Charms, Spells & Formulas* is $27.80 cash-with-order. This price includes postage and handling within the United States. Minnesota residents must add 6.5% sales tax. For additional quantities, please order in multiples of five. For Canadian and foreign orders, add postage and handling charges as above. Credit card (VISA, MasterCard, American Express) orders are accepted. Charge card orders only ($15.00 minimum order) may be phoned in free within the U.S.A. or Canada by dialing 1-800-THE-MOON. For customer service, call 1-612-291-1970. Mail orders to:

LLEWELLYN PUBLICATIONS
P.O. Box 64383-L501, St. Paul, MN 55164-0383, U.S.A.

Prices subject to change without notice.

EARTH POWER
Techniques of Natural Magic
by Scott Cunningham

Magick is the art of working with the forces of Nature to bring about necessary and desired, changes. The forces of Nature—expressed through Earth, Air, Fire and Water—are our "spiritual ancestors" who paved the way for our emergence from the prehistoric seas of creation. Attuning to and working with these energies in magick not only lends you the power to affect changes in your life, it also allows you to sense your own place in the larger scheme of Nature. Using the "Old Ways" enables you to live a better life and to deepen your understanding of the world. The tools and powers of magick are around you, waiting to be grasped and utilized. This book gives you the means to put Magick into your life, shows you how to make and use the tools, and gives you spells for every purpose

0-87542-121-0, 176 pgs., 5-1/4 x 8, illus., softcover $9.95

PRACTICAL COLOR MAGICK
by Raymond Buckland, Ph.D.

Color magick is powerful—and safe. Here is a sourcebook for the psychic influence of color on our physical lives. Contains complete rituals and meditations for practical applications of color magick for health, success and love. Find full instructions on how to meditate more effectively and use color to stimulate the chakras and unfold psychic abilities. Learn to use color in divination and in the making of talismans, sigils and magick squares.

This book will teach all the powers of light and more. You'll learn new forms of expression of your innermost self, new ways of relating to others with the secret languages of light and color. Put true color back into your life with the rich spectrum of ideas and practical magical formulas from *Practical Color Magick!*

0-87542-047-8, 160 pgs., illus., softcover $6.95

Prices subject to change without notice.

THE LLEWELLYN PRACTICAL GUIDE TO CREATIVE VISUALIZATION
For the Fulfillment of Your Desires
by Denning & Phillips

IF YOU CAN SEE IT ... in your Mind's Eye ... you will have it! It's true: you can have whatever you want, but there are "laws" to mental creation that must be followed. The power of the mind is not limited to, nor limited by, the material world. *Creative Visualization* enables Man to reach beyond, into the invisible world of Astral and Spiritual Forces.Some people apply this innate power without actually knowing what they are doing, and achieve great success and happiness; most people, however, use this same power, again unknowingly, incorrectly, and experience bad luck, failure, or at best an unfulfilled life.

This book changes that. Through an easy series of step-by-step, progressive exercises, your mind is applied to bring desire into realization! Wealth, power, success, happiness even psychic powers ... even what we call magickal power and spiritual attainment ... all can be yours. You can easily develop this completely natural power, and correctly apply it, for your immediate and practical benefit. Illustrated with unique, "puts-you-into-the-picture" visualization aids.
0-87542-183-0, 294 pgs., 5-1/4 x 8, illus., softcover $8.95

THE LLEWELLYN PRACTICAL GUIDE TO PSYCHIC SELF-DEFENSE AND WELL-BEING
by Denning & Phillips

Psychic well-being and psychic self-defense are two sides of the same coin, just as are physical health and resistance to disease. Each person (and every living thing) is surrounded by an electromagnetic force field, or AURA, that can provide the means to psychic self-defense and to dynamic well-being. This book explores the world of very real "psychic warfare" of which we are all victims.

Every person in our modern world is subjected to psychic stress and psychological bombardment: advertising promotions that play upon primitive emotions, political and religious appeals that work on feelings of insecurity and guilt, noise, threats of violence and war, news of crime and disaster, etc.

This book shows the nature of psychic attacks—ranging from actual acts of black magic to bitter jealousy and hate—and the reality of psychic stress, the structure of the psyche and its interrelationship with the physical body. It shows how each person must develop his weakened aura into a powerful defense-shield, thereby gaining both physical protection and energetic well-being that can extend to protection from physical violence, accidents ... even ill health.
0-87542-190-3, 306 pgs., 5 1/4 x 8, illus., softcover $9.95

CUNNINGHAM'S ENCYCLOPEDIA OF MAGICAL HERBS
by Scott Cunningham

This is the most comprehensive source of herbal data for magical uses ever printed! Almost every one of the over 400 herbs are illustrated, making this a great source for herb identification. For each herb you will also find: magical properties, planetary rulerships, genders, associated deities, folk and Latin names and much more. To make this book even easier to use, it contains a folk name cross reference, and all of the herbs are fully indexed. There is also a large annotated bibliography, and a list of mail order suppliers so you can find the books and herbs you need. Like all of Cunningham's books, this one does not require you to use complicated rituals or expensive magical paraphernalia. Instead, it shares with you the intrinsic powers of the herbs. Thus, you will be able to discover which herbs, by their very nature, can be used for luck, love, success, money, divination, astral projection, safety, psychic self-defense and much more. Besides being interesting and educational it is also fun, and fully illustrated with unusual woodcuts from old herbals. This book has rapidly become the classic in its field. It enhances books such as 777 and is a must for all Wiccans.

0-87542-122-9, 336 pgs., 6 x 9, illus., softcover   **$12.95**

MAGICAL HERBALISM
The Secret Craft of the Wise
by Scott Cunningham

Certain plants are prized for the special range of energies—the vibrations, or powers—they possess. *Magical Herbalism* unites the powers of plants and man to produce, and direct, change in accord with human will and desire.

This is Magic that is beautiful and natural—a Craft of Hand and Mind merged with the Power and Glory of Nature: a special kind that does not use the medicinal powers of herbs, but rather the subtle vibrations and scents that touch the psychic centers and stir the astral field in which we live to work at the causal level behind the material world.

This is the Magic of Enchantment . . . of word and gesture to shape the images of mind and channel the energies of the herbs. It is a Magic for everyone—for the herbs are easily and readily obtained, the tools are familiar or easily made, and the technology that of home and garden. This book includes step-by-step guidance to the preparation of herbs and to their compounding in incense and oils, sachets and amulets, simples and infusions, with simple rituals and spells for every purpose.

0-87542-120-2, 260 pgs., 5-¼ x 8, illus., softcover   **$9.95**

PRACTICAL CANDLEBURNING RITUALS
Spells & Rituals for Every Purpose
by Raymond Buckland, Ph.D.

Magick is a way in which to apply the full range of your hidden psychic powers to the problems we all face in daily life. We know that normally we use only 5 per cent of our total powers. Magick taps powers from deep inside our psyche where we are in contact with the Universe's limitless resources.

Magick need not be complex—it can be as simple as using a few candles to focus your mind, a simple ritual to give direction to your desire, a few words to give expression to your wish.This book shows you how easy it can be. Here is Magick for fun, Magick as a Craft, Magick for Success. Love, Luck, Money, Marriage, Healing; Magick to stop slander, to learn truth, to heal an unhappy marriage, to overcome a bad habit, to break up a love affair, etc.

Magick—with nothing fancier than ordinary candles, and the 28 rituals in this book (given in both Christian and Old Religion versions)—can transform your life.

0-87542-048-6, 208 pgs., 5-¼ x 8, illus., softcover $6.95

BUCKLAND'S COMPLETE GYPSY FORTUNETELLER
by Raymond Buckland

Buckland's Complete Gypsy Fortuneteller gives you everything you need to perform divination in the Gypsy tradition. Included is the book *Secrets of Gypsy Fortunetelling,* in which the secrets of divination with palms, tea leaves, cards, dice and other methods are revealed.

You can use the insights gained from the book to perform powerful divination with The Buckland Gypsy Fortunetelling Deck. This 74-card deck has a distinctive Romani (Gypsy) Major Arcana, and a Minor Arcana composed of a regular poker deck. A handy 16" x 24" four-color layout sheet is included, making the deck instantly and easily usable. Each side illustrates a different layout:the Seven Star layout and the Romani Star layout. With this you can discover future events, hopes, fears, strengths and much more.

All of these attractive and useful items are packaged neatly into a convenient box. A one-of-a-kind kit that makes a surprising and intriguing gift, *Buckland's Complete Fortuneteller* reflects the nuances of Gypsy culture while bringing a potential for improvement in anybody's life.

0-87542-055-9, book, 74-card deck, layout sheet $24.95

THE LLEWELLYN ANNUALS

Llewellyn's MOON SIGN BOOK: Approximately 500 pages of valuable information on gardening, fishing, weather, stock market forecasts, personal horoscopes, good planting dates, and general instructions for finding the best date to do just about anything! Articles by prominent forecasters and writers in the fields of gardening, astrology, politics, economics and cycles. This special almanac, different from any other, has been published annually since 1906. It's fun, informative and has been a great help to millions in their daily planning. New larger 5-1/4 x 8 format. **State year $6.95**

Llewellyn's SUN SIGN BOOK: Your personal horoscope for the entire year! All 12 signs are included in one handy book. Also included are forecasts, special feature articles, and an action guide for each sign. Monthly horoscopes are written by Gloria Star, author of *Optimum Child*, for your personal sun sign and there are articles on a variety of subjects written by well-known astrologers from around the country. Much more than just a horoscope guide! Entertaining and fun the year around. New larger 5 /4 x 8 format. **State year $6.95**

Llewellyn's DAILY PLANETARY GUIDE: Includes all of the major daily aspects plus their exact times in Eastern and Pacific time zones, lunar phases, signs and voids plus their times, planetary motion, a monthly ephemeris, sunrise and sunset tables, special articles on the planets, signs, aspects, a business guide, planetary hours, rulerships, and much more. Large 5-1/4 x 8 format for more writing space, spiral bound to lie flat, address and phone listings, time-zone conversion chart and blank horoscope chart. **State year $9.95**

Llewellyn's ASTROLOGICAL POCKET PLANNER: Daily Ephemeris & Aspectarian: Designed to slide easily into a purse or briefcase, this all-new annual is jam-packed with those dates and planetary information astrologers need when forecasting future events. Comes with a regular calendar section, a smaller section for projecting dates into the year ahead, a 3-year ephemeris, a listing of planetary aspects, a planetary associations chart, a time-zone chart and retrograde table. **State year $7.95**

Llewellyn's MAGICAL ALMANAC: This beautifully illustrated almanac explores traditional earth religions and folklore while focusing on magical myths. Each month is summarized in a two-page format with information that includes the phases of the moon, festivals and rites for the month, as well as detailed magical advice. This is an indispensable guide is for anyone who is interested in planning rituals, spells and other magical advice. It features writing by some of the most prominent authors in the field. **State year $6.95**

CUNNINGHAM'S ENCYCLOPEDIA OF CRYSTAL, GEM & METAL MAGIC
by Scott Cunningham
Here you will find the most complete information anywhere on the magical qualities of more than 100 crystals and gemstones as well as several metals. The information for each crystal, gem or metal includes: its related energy, planetary rulership, magical element, deities, Tarot Card, and the magical powers that each is believed to possess. Also included is a complete description of their uses for magical purposes. The classic on the subject.
0-87542-126-1, 240 pgs., 6 x 9, illus., color plates, softcover $14.95

THE MAGICAL HOUSEHOLD
Empower Your Home with Love, Protection, Health & Happiness
by Scott Cunningham and David Harrington
Whether your home is a small apartment or a palatial mansion, you want it to be something special. Now it can be with *The Magical Household*. Learn how to make your home more than just a place to live. Turn it into a place of security, life, fun and magic. Here you will not find the complex magic of the ceremonial magician. Rather, you will learn simple, quick and effective magical spells that use nothing more than common items in your house: furniture, windows, doors, carpet, pets, etc. You will learn to take advantage of the intrinsic power and energy that is already in your home, waiting to be tapped. You will learn to make magic a part of your life. The result is a home that is safeguarded from harm and a place which will bring you happiness, health and more.
0-87542-124-5, 208 pgs., 5-1/4 x 8, illus., softcover $8.95

SECRETS OF GYPSY FORTUNETELLING
by Ray Buckland
This book unveils the Romani secrets of fortunetelling, explaining in detail the many different methods used by these nomads. For generations they have survived on their skills as seers. Their accuracy is legendary. They are a people who seem to be born with "the sight" … the ability to look into the past, present and future using only the simplest of tools to aid them. The methods of divination presented in this book are all practical methods—no expensive or hard-to-get items are necessary. The Gypsies are accomplished at using natural objects and everyday items to serve them in their endeavors: Sticks and stones, knives and needles, cards and dice. Using these non-complex objects, and following the traditional Gypsy ways shown, you can become a seer and improve the quality of your own life and of these lives around you.
0-87542-051-6, 240 pgs., mass market, illus. $4.99

A VICTORIAN GRIMOIRE
by Patricia Telesco

Like a special opportunity to rummage through your grandmother's attic, *A Victorian Grimoire* offers you a personal invitation to discover a storehouse of magical treasures. Enhance every aspect of your daily life as you begin to reclaim the romance, simplicity and "know-how" of the Victorian era—that exceptional period of American history when people's lives and times were shaped by their love of the land, of home and family, and by their simple acceptance of magic as part of everyday life.

More and more, people are searching for ways to create peace and beauty in this increasingly chaotic world. This special handbook—*Grimoire*—shows you how to recreate that peace and beauty with simple, down-to-earth "Victorian Enchantments" that turn every mundane act into an act of magic . . . from doing the dishes . . . to making beauty-care products . . . to creating games for children. This book is a handy reference when you need a specific spell, ritual, recipe or tincture for any purpose. What's more, *A Victorian Grimoire* is a captivating study of the turn of the century and a comprehensive repository of common-sense knowledge. Learn how to relieve a backache, dry and store herbs, help children get over fears of the dark, treat pets with first aid, and much, much more.

0-87542-784-7, 368 pgs., 7 x 10, illus., softcover   **$14.95**

TAROT SPELLS
by Janina Renee

This book provides a means of recognizing and affirming one's own personal power through use of the Tarot. With the practical advice and beautiful illustrations in this book, the reader can perform spells for:Influencing dreams, Better health, Legal matters, Better family relations, Beating addiction, Finding a job, Better gardening and more. Thirty-five areas of life are discussed, and spells are provided which address specific issues in these areas.

The reader uses Tarot layouts in combination with affirmations and visualizations to obtain a desired result. Many spells can be used with color, gemstones or magical tools to assist the reader in focusing his or her desire.

Graced with beautiful card illustrations from the Robin Wood Tarot, this book can be used immediately even by those who don't own a Tarot deck. No previous experience with the Tarot is necessary. Those familiar with the Tarot can gain new insights into the symbolism of their own particular deck.

0-87542-670-0, 288 pgs., 6 x 9, illus., softcover   **$12.95**